Jean Barthel

Sources
of Information
in Librarianship
and
Information
Science

2nd Edition

Sources of Information in Librarianship and Information Science

2nd Edition

Ray Prytherch

Gower

Aldershot · Brookfield USA · Hong Kong · Singapore · Sydney

First Published 1983
Second edition 1987

Gower Publishing Company Limited
Gower House
Croft Road
Aldershot
Hants GU11 3HR
England

Gower Publishing Company
Old Post Road
Brookfield
Vermont 05036
USA

British Library Cataloguing in Publication Data
Prytherch, R. J.
  Sources of information in librarianship and
  information science. —— 2nd ed.
  1. Library science —— 2nd ed.
  2. Library science —— Information services
  I. Title
020′.7   Z666

Library of Congress Cataloging-in-Publication Data
Prytherch, Raymond John.
  Sources of information in librarianship and
information science.

  Bibliography: p.
  Includes index.
  1. Library science —— Bibliography 2. Bibliography ——
Bibliography —— Library science. 3. Library science ——
Information services ——. 4. Information science ——
Bibliography. 5. Bibliography —— Bibliography ——
Information science. 6. Information science ——
Information services. I. Title.
Z666.P935   1987   016.02   87–8637

ISBN 0 566 05509 0

Printed and bound in Great Britain by
Biddles Ltd, Guildford and King's Lynn

Contents

Preface

The first edition of this book sold remarkably successfully, and generated several appreciative reviews and much interesting correspondence. Given the rate at which the traditional bases of the profession have changed, a new edition was clearly necessary. As with the previous edition, so here I have been brief and intend the book only as an introductory guide.

Professional literature is still growing in quantity; the development of any profession depends upon the absorption of existing knowledge both to consolidate good practice and create new initiatives. By these means service to our clientele is ultimately enhanced. This book is aimed at providing clues to finding our way into the literature quickly, effectively and efficiently.

I have retained the structure of the first edition, updating material where necessary, substituting new information and introducing several new sources. I am once again grateful to friends, colleagues, correspondents, editors and publishers for their comments and help; and in particular to the staff of the Study and Demonstration Unit at the Department of Library and Information Studies, Leeds Polytechnic.

Ray Prytherch
Lomond
Scotland Lane
Horsforth
December 1986

Figures

Formal acknowledgements are given here for the reproduction of copyright material.

Chapter 5

Figure 5.1   *Bibliographic Index*, prefatory note. Copyright © 1986, by the H.W. Wilson Company. Reproduced by permission.

Figure 5.2   *Bibliographic Index*, vol. 25, 1985, p. 317. Copyright © 1985, 1986 by the H.W. Wilson Company. Reproduced by permission.

Chapter 6

Figure 6.1   *LISA* 1986, p. 364. Reproduced by permission of Library Association Publishing Ltd.

Figure 6.2   *LISA*, 1986, p. clvii. Reproduced by permission of Library Association Publishing Ltd.

Figure 6.3   *Library literature*, December 1985, p. iii. Copyright © 1985/6 by the H.W. Wilson company. Reproduced by permission.

Figure 6.4   *Library literature*, December 1985, p. 93. Copyright © 1985/6 by the H.W. Wilson Company. Reproduced by permission.

Figure 6.5   *Library literature*, December 1985, p. 73. Copyright © 1985/6 by the H.W. Wilson Company. Reproduced by permission.

Figure 6.6   *Informatics Abstracts*, vol. 23, no. 12, 1985. p. 58. Copyright © 1985, VINITI, Moscow.

Figure 6.7   *Informatics Abstracts*, vol. 23, no. 12, 1985, p. 1. Copyright © 1985, VINITI, Moscow.

Figure 6.8   *Informatics Abstracts*, vol. 23, no. 12, 1985, p. 136. Copyright © 1985, VINITI, Moscow.

Figure 6.9   *Information Science Abstracts*, vol. 21, 1986. Introduction. Copyright © 1986 by IFI/Plenum Data Company.

Figure 6.10   *Information Science Abstracts*, vol. 21, 1986, p. 263. Copyright © 1986 by IFI/Plenum Data Company.

Chapter 7

Figure 7.1   *British Education Index*, 1985, p. 219.

Figure 7.2   *Resources in Education*, vol. 20, no. 12, December, 1985 p. 104.

Figure 7.3   *Resources in Education*, vol. 20, no. 12, December, 1985 p. viii.

Figure 7.4   *Resources in Education*, vol. 20, no. 12, December, 1985, p. 211.

Chapter 8

Figure 8.1   *General Information Programme/UNISIST Newsletter*, vol. 14, no. 1, 1986, cover page. Reproduced with acknowledgement to Unesco.

Figure 8.2   *R. & D. Projects in Documentation and Librarianship*, vol. 16, no. 2. cover page.

1   Introduction

This book follows the pattern of the previous edition in being brief and practical. It is written on the assumption that the reader will want to *use* it, not to digest it from theoretical interest. It is a guide to the sources of information in the professional fields of librarianship and information science and the peripheral areas that these terms now embrace. Whilst one might expect members of these professions by definition to have expertise greater than that of other professions, in fact there is a lack of familiarity with the full range of sources, and a lack of knowledge about their coverage and characteristics.

This is not a learned guide; it puts no emphasis on the more obscure areas of little current general interest, although the sources described will lead the researcher to appropriate information if they are used thoroughly. It tends to concentrate on English-language material, which has been shown to comprise over 70 per cent of the accessible professional literature (Bottle and Efthimiadis, 1984), although again sources in other major languages are covered by the services we shall discuss.

It is written for practising librarians and information workers, who find a need for enhancing their professional awareness in order to develop new services, to explore new areas of work in an unfavourable job market, and to compare, assess and evaluate their own or their unit's effectiveness in a wider context. Many are now turning to personal research, and to deeper exploration of the profession both to keep abreast of new advances in technology and to find interest and satisfaction in their jobs when career development is frustrated.

Training of professional and non-professional staff is of increasing importance in depressed times, but trainers find themselves under greater pressure than most in economic uncertainties; this book should provide trainers and training officers with ideas and practical assistance in planning and preparing training, in finding which areas have been well covered in other services, and who could offer advice and expertise.

Staff of schools of librarianship and information science have a similar need for information for professional and teaching development, or for personal or institutional research, and there may be material that is unfamiliar to some. Certainly students on professional courses or entering the profession should find this an essential guide for discovering information to further that study, for career planning, for interview preparation, as well as for general professional curiosity and awareness.

The plan of the book is to define the subject area which it covers in some detail, and to consider the patterns of publication. This will lead to a discussion of a strategy for searching the literature. The greater part of the book is devoted to the principal services which provide access to the literature and professional knowledge in general, and this section is illustrated with sample entries.

Minor sources of information are examined more discursively, and the final chapter is intended to assist in identifying the means of keeping up to date with professional developments.

Most of the printed services discussed are available online and on compact disk (CD-ROM). The format of the service, and the technique of assembling terms and adjusting them, is valid for any version of the same service: therefore it is entirely reasonable to concentrate here on the printed format, and allow readers to transfer the information to the online form where this is to be used.

2   A definition of the subject area

The *Library and Information Services Council* in its paper *Professional education and training for library and information work: a review* (Office of Arts and Libraries, 1985) comments on the wide range of skills now appropriate to the profession: these include such disparate roles as authorship, editing, printing, primary publishing, document delivery, collection management, conservation, database and catalogue production, thesaurus construction, system design and management, online computing and searching, the management of resources, records and archives, information analysis and repackaging, question and answer services, marketing, research, advice, brokerage, signposting and referral, exhibitions and consultancy.

The sources and services to be described cover between them all these fields, but may be supplemented by services in kindred areas. Information can be traced about any type of library, any category of user, any type of process, routine or activity in any part of the world. Although some services specialize in particular areas, most are not narrow in their coverage of topics. Information can thus be found relating to public libraries in general and to their specialized services, to academic libraries of all types – university, polytechnic, college or school, to industrial, commercial, legal, medical and any other 'special' libraries and information units, to information services outside the conventional network of libraries, to national and government libraries of most countries, and to processes within these services, from conservation to automation.

The quantity of literature relating to the users of libraries and information units and their needs, demands, and assessment of what is provided is very small compared to that written from the providers' viewpoint; what is published can be traced through the services covered here, as well as some which is semi-published. A much greater quantity of material is written about technical processes and routines, and this can be readily traced.

The principal services began at a stage in the professsion's history before the most recent expansion in publishing; consequently, although the services have developed and expanded, their topic coverage is still all-embracing. Whilst there is now a great diversity between various parts of the profession, between a rare book librarian and a community outreach librarian, for example, or a school librarian and an information consultant in industry, and despite the dichotomy of professional qualifications, all practitioners would come to the same services in looking for further professional information in their fields.

Most parts of the profession have been subject to a rapid development in recent years; research has become common, and technical developments have had an enormous impact. The move towards a graduate profession and full-time professional education should be leading to more ideas and developments; certainly the extent of professional literature has grown, the number of conferences and the publications thereby generated demonstrate increased cerebral activity, and the aware professional will need to find the way through the research and the publications, and to evaluate their relevance.

Economic constraints on libraries and information units provide a further need for information; evaluative work on the efficiency and effectiveness of services, means of coping with closures and depleted funds, information on concepts, products, and techniques, which must be up to date, reliable, and not passed on by a salesman.

While the professional literature has developed in response to professional change, an equally essential change has brought into the profession's field a number of fringe topics that are to many practitioners and educators every bit as important as the traditional topics of librarianship and information work; larger local government units, the incorporation of libraries within leisure services or education directorates, and the massive size of national and some university libraries involve their staffs in a detailed understanding of national and local government practice; depleted funds demand a greater expertise in financial planning and accounting; the need to justify the continuation or development of services involves the ability to use evaluative techniques; statistical information has to be

compiled, collated and interpreted; computers demand an understanding of their operations, limitations and possibilities. The
professional librarian or information specialist is a manager: concepts
and practices of management have to be mastered, staffing policies
prepared, personnel records kept, training organized and evaluated,
the psychology of the workforce understood. Competence in some of
these areas is now a requirement of many professional posts. These are
the areas least well handled by the principal services described here,
and we shall additionally range over a number of sources that seem at
first to have little relevance to traditional librarianship.

Further pressures lead to a greater need for professional
information: librarians and information workers need to explore new
areas of work, and investigate new techniques. A static job-market
may lead to internal re-allocation of responsibilities; evaluation of
services may suggest new groups of users, new types of activity. The
wider the field to be examined, the greater the extent of the literature,
and the greater the need to make a fast, economical and accurate
search for established sources and examples of comparable
development.

Staffing contractions call for economies of technique, more
intensive staff training, the exploitation of computerized systems, and
the understanding of, and adjustment to, institutional change.

In professional education, the economic difficulties facing
schools of librarianship are forcing a contraction of staff,
redeployment into new areas of professional teaching and courses that
cover more than the traditional topics. Research activity has become
an expected part of most schools' work, and many projects demand
supervision in unfamiliar areas, the employment of non-librarians to
cover educational, statistical or other aspects of a project, and a great
need generally to understand the paths into the professional literature.
Postgraduate and undergraduate students also now need to develop
their competence in searching professional literature to support a
greater reliance on project work – part of a general educational move
towards student-centred learning, the active rather than passive
approach. Within many schools there are part-time courses for the
enhancement of qualifications, and students on such courses, together
with staff undergoing organized training, will need to search the
literature thoroughly for basic information in new areas, and to locate
current developmental work.

For basic definitions of terms there are sources which provide concise summaries: the most current of these is the sixth edition of the *Librarian's Glossary and Reference Book* (Gower Publishing Co., 1986). Still generally known as *Harrod's Glossary*, this source provides brief definitions and explanations of terms in printing, the book trade, bookbinding, archive work, technical processes, computer operation, database management, professional activities, international organizations and much else, incorporating acronyms and abbreviations, and abundant cross references. This makes an ideal starting point for terminological enquiries. A second such volume is G.A. Glaister's *Glaister's glossary of the book* (2nd ed., Allen and Unwin, 1979) subtitled: 'Terms used in papermaking, printing, bookbinding and publishing with notes on illuminated manuscripts and private presses'. This glossary became a standard work soon after its first appearance in 1960 and comprises some 4,000 entries within its specialized fields, which, although outside the main areas of our subject, are sufficiently close to it to make the work a useful tool. Definitions vary in length from a brief sentence to a column or more, and there are illustrations of several technical processes and machines. Included as appendices are specimen typefaces, Latin place names used as imprints on early printed books, proof correction symbols and a bibliography. For terms within its field this glossary can be highly recommended. John Feather's *Dictionary of book history* (Croom Helm, 1986) covers a similar range of topics. Further works which provide definitions of terms and explanations of acronyms and technical vocabulary include B. Buchanan's *Glossary of indexing terms* (Bingley, 1976), which gives over 900 entries with full definitions, and the *Bookman's glossary*, edited by J. Peters (6th ed., Bowker, 1983) – a short, concise guide recording American usage. For converting technical terms between languages the standard works include Elsevier's *Dictionary of library science, information and documentation* edited by W.E. Clason (Elsevier, 1976), which is arranged on an English alphabetical basis and covers terms in English/American, French, Spanish, Italian, Dutch and German. This also includes an Arabic supplement. Secondly there is the *Librarian's practical dictionary in twenty-two languages*, 7th ed., edited by Z. Pipics (Verlag Dokumentation, 1977) – this uses English as the base language, while earlier editions have used others. A similar publication is the *Terminology of Documentation*, compiled by G. Wersig and U. Nevelling (Unesco, 1976), which features 1,200 basic terms in five languages including Russian. There are indexes in all five of the languages, and an index arranged by UDC numbers.

For the expansion of acronyms, initialisms and abbreviations, a current source is A.C. Montgomery's *Acronyms and abbreviations in library and information work* (3rd ed., Library Association, 1986), and this could be supplemented by Pauline Vaillancourt's *International directory of acronyms in library, information and computer sciences* (Bowker, 1980) or by R. Tayyeb and K. Chandna's *Dictionary of acronyms in library and information science*, 2nd ed. (Canadian Library Association, 1985), and in a more limited context by Richard Hipgrave's *Computing terms and acronyms: a dictionary* (Library Association, 1985), which is very thorough in its area, and includes expansions of many database acronyms.

3   The nature of the literature

As we have discussed, the range of activities covered within this profession has proliferated; this has been reflected in the expansion of professional literature both in range and quantity. Ali (1985) identifies *academic* (research type) literature, and *practitioner* literature: the former reflects the enormous growth of research due to the need to establish status, to avoid professional stagnation, and the greater availability of institutional and other funding agencies. (Krausse and Sieburth (1985) point to the growing pressure on US academic librarians to publish material in their campaign to rate faculty status.) *Practitioner* literature tends to be based almost entirely on description and discussion of the authors' experiences, and is particularly valuable in 'newer' areas, such as database searching, and automation; *RQ*, *Vine* and *Program* would exemplify this category of output.

Historically professional literature has been much criticized; in the early 1960s Eric Moon, then editor of *Library Journal*, commented on dullness and duplication: he accused the library press of being short on new ideas, but long on dullness, superfluity, repetition and plagiarism (Moon, 1961). A few years later he expanded his complaints with a typical forcefulness: was much that was published worth the time and effort? was it communicating anything that anyone wanted to know? was it published merely to establish and maintain an identity, and was that identity one that we wanted to live with? He argued that worthwhile material was diverted into obscure places, while unimportant matter took over the major journals; in nine years of editing *Library Journal* he claimed that almost everything he rejected was published elsewhere (Moon, 1969).

Moon was maybe thinking mainly of the US scene, but equally in the UK a decade later the same type of proliferation was seen; Graham Jones felt that the 'incredible stream of garbage' was an apt description of the British press too (Jones, 1976), and Joan Gresham has analysed the current position in some detail; she points to the fragmentation of the literature, parallel to the creation of new professional groupings, and the stratification of the profession, with a radical alternative press appearing in competition with the established presses and journals (Gresham, 1979). She also identifies the phenomenon of ritualistic publication: professional groups feel bound to produce a journal, where in many cases a simpler, unpretentious newsletter would be more appropriate. Gresham interprets from the journal literature three features of the modern profession: firstly that an enormous gulf now separates many members of the same group of workers – a public librarian involved in community profiling will find little common ground with the technical services librarian in a university, although both are 'librarians'; secondly that newer groupings are keen to make common cause with analogous groups outside the profession, for example in the worlds of computing, politics or sex; and thirdly that journal articles have ceased to be 'practical', and moved into the style of the 'theoretic treatise'. This naturally mirrors the switch of professional education to full-time schools, away from the UK pattern of the 1930s where the journal provided a commentary on the recognized syllabus.

Sam Goldstein has been a most outspoken critic of the attitudes of librarians towards their own literature: to him the lack of use made of the available material is a damning indictment of the potential readers not of the literature itself (Goldstein, 1979). He claims that it doesn't matter how many journals there are, since very few are read anyway, certainly by working librarians; thus the information explosion is a problem only to library school librarians; the quality may be poor, maybe it is uninspiring and 'stinks', but this is true of other fields too, and it is after all the information that is wanted, not style or entertainment; everything is relevant to somebody, and intellectual curiosity may be sparked off by an odd comment more than by a stylish paragraph, therefore the charge of irrelevance will not stick; is much of it a rehash? Well, since we each do so little reading who is qualified to say: knowledge is presumed to be the development and improvement of other people's work and a certain degree of repetition is probably inevitable. Goldstein concludes that a study of the literature 'ought to be a core subject in library schools', and we may suggest that, if it were, then much of the repetition could be avoided, and a lesser effort by the reader could bring a far greater return in information.

Other commentators disagree; Stevens (1984) notes many positive features of the literature: it proves that we are capable of research, that we can write with clarity, use a professional perspective, and make a contribution to other fields of study. He argues that proliferation implies maturity, that the refereeing process is now ensuring a better quality, and that the existence of a quantity of material demonstrates that we have the resources and incentives to publish.

Growth in quantity is not of course unique; librarianship and information science are following patterns that have been seen in other subject areas. Analysis of citation habits suggests that Bradford's law of scatter can be seen to operate – Alan Gilchrist believed that there was a strong core of material, but 'a huge tail of comparatively unproductive journals' (Gilchrist, 1966). This dispersion could be due to the role of information handling as a service function, lacking definition, as Dansey has suggested (Dansey, 1973), and the pattern of citations places information science nearer to the social sciences and humanities than to the natural sciences: it is a 'soft science', showing less than ten citations per article on average, and much cited material is reports and monographs. A later study (Peritz, 1981) confirmed that the level of citation from sources in the same field is very high (about 80 per cent) leaving only 20 per cent from sources outside the profession: this is an odd ratio for an applied subject and disturbingly introspective.

Straightforward book publishing used to be an easily controlled business, in the hands of a small number of big-name firms; in the last thirty years this pattern has changed as markedly in our subject fields as in any other. There has been an expansion of the near-print business, particularly in the US, and small commercial presses such as *Oryx*, *Scarecrow* and *Shoestring* have become household names.

Others have also entered the monograph publishing world in earnest; professional associations have included this activity in their role, with varying views of their commercial interest and professional responsibility. Schools of librarianship have begun to publish monographs, mainly so far in the US, using the parent publishing house of their university. British schools have not so far entered this market; their publications are mainly reports of research. Late in the day libraries themselves have realized that they have the material and the means to publish books of value to the profession. In the main, despite the impetus given by the need to raise income from any source, publishing by libraries is embryonic, and its impact on the professional press is small. In 1975 Taylor, examining British books on library science, found 62 of UK trade origin, 19 of US trade origin, no fewer than 36 from professional associations, 14 of government origin, and 18 ascribed to libraries (Taylor, 1977). This list obscures the true picture to some extent: textbooks tend to come from established publishers, while descriptive accounts of new buildings, new services and historical perspectives tend to come from libraries.

Whatever the proliferation of monograph publishing, a greater expansion by far has come to the journal market; over the last forty years there has been a startling increase in the number of titles published. The Library Association's *Library and Information Bulletin* recorded in 1970 a total of 564 journals received by the LA Library (Library Association, 1970/1971/1974); in 1971 a further 118 were added, and in 1974 another listing recorded 140 more. Sam Goldstein identified 835, as a minimum total covered by the leading abstracting services (Goldstein, 1973). LaBorie, Halperin and White (1985), examining coverage of the literature by the abstracting and indexing services, calculate that 1,210 relevant journal titles were available; Bottle and Efthimiadis (1984) identify 1,391 titles, and comment that it would be defensible to raise that total to 1,545 journals, based on examination of published serial bibliographies.

For those keen to join in supplying material to these journals N.D. and N.B. Stevens' *Authors' guide to journals in library and information science* (Haworth Press, 1982) lists some 140 US and UK journals with standardized data on their requirements for authors wishing to submit articles.

A detailed survey of British librarianship and information science journals was produced by Norman Roberts (Roberts, 1979); the total of British journals then stood at over sixty, mostly with a small circulation, many of special interest only and not commercially based. He categorizes material into *primary journals* – scholarly in style, and with a high rejection rate of articles; *secondary* – more popular in style but still general in coverage; *official journals*, being the output of various professional associations, and the corresponding *alternative journals* produced to counteract the effect of the establishment titles; *special-interest journals*, of which there are now many under the Library Association umbrella alone; and *in-house journals*, productions for example of the various parts of the British Library. The modest increase in number of British journals alone represented a greater complexity of professional communication, and economic difficulties and market forces caused some to go to the wall and others (like the *Library Association Record* itself) to change their style dramatically.

In addition to the proliferation of publishers and journals, there are many other publishing channels open that simply did not exist thirty years ago; in the main these channels are connected with schools of librarianship and information science. Research has become a part of our professional life: it tends to be centred on the schools, and the outcome of research is generally if not inevitably a report of some description. These may be published by the school, by the individual author, or by a sponsoring body. Also within the schools large-scale projects, dissertations and theses are produced, and many are published, or, more awkwardly, semi-published – made available but not advertised or sold through normal channels. In North America the theses produced in the schools number several hundred a year and, whilst the general standard is uneven, some are worthwhile reading.

Libraries also publish reports of research, development or other activity. These may range from large-scale programmes, such as those of the British Library, to small single items from individual authorities. In professional associations and government departments reports, policy statements and situation summaries are prepared, and a surprisingly large proportion of these are not reprinted in journals and newsletters, but remain semi-published.

Publication is therefore a haphazard business: Taylor in 1971 reckoned that over 6,000 documents per year were produced relevant to our subject fields (Taylor, 1971). The growth of those fields, the increasing lack of clarity at the edges, and the further expansion of publishing will have enormously increased that: Bottle and Efthimiadis (1984) calculated that at the time of their article there could be 500,000 documents published relevant to the profession. Marco (1983) reckons on over 15,000 *articles* per year.

Yet despite all this, it remains inevitable that much work goes unrecorded: key people in particular subjects may not write reports or articles, or their articles may be rejected and filed in desk drawers. 'Invisible colleges' of people concerned with similar problems meet to discuss developments and may produce more worthwhile information on a given topic in an afternoon's discussion than a researcher can discover in all the available literature. Whatever we may hope or plan to do to control information, we shall be unable ever to contain it with 100 per cent reliability.

We have concentrated so far on information in the form of the printed word; clearly, though, the 'literature' of librarianship and information science includes a number of audio and visual productions. These formats pose problems additional to those outlined above, and the solutions to them are partial and imperfect.

Many audio-visual packages and videotapes are available introducing libraries in general, specific libraries, specific services or books, or the literature of a subject field. In the UK there have been video productions from the Open University introducing their students to library resources, teaching materials from the Council for Educational Technology, and a series of slide/tapes produced for SCONUL by twenty or more British academic libraries.

Most material is *user*-orientated, and therefore used by the librarian or information worker to aid his clients rather than assist his own information need, but obviously the two demands are closely intertwined. There are, however, many productions whose purpose is to educate library school students, or to facilitate in-service training. Individual libraries have produced some material for these purposes, but the schools themselves have produced much more; in the UK the College of Librarianship Wales and the Leeds Polytechnic School have been particularly active. The North American equivalents would be more numerous: Joseph Palmer has written a most detailed synopsis of non-print media in our subject area, and ends his paper, which names dozens of individual items, with a full annotated bibliography of selection aids (Palmer, 1979). The British Universities Film and Video Council has recently (1985) issued *Librarianship: a select audiovisual resource list*.

A peculiarly US market (and problem) is the audio- and video-taping of conference papers and discussions. The technical quality and lack of editing makes these productions a very awkward area for libraries to enter with a view to purchase. It is in such a case as this that the bigger problem presented by non-print material really matters: the lack of any reliable review source for our subject field. *ASIS Journal* has a regular review section for non-print items, but elsewhere coverage is occasional and haphazard. With materials that are generally expensive and difficult to obtain other than by outright purchase, this is a fundamental problem. So far as possible in this book, we shall treat non-print materials in the same way as any other 'ordinary' item; the abstracting services cover these items, but we need to recognize the basic problem of inadequate bibliographical control which renders any secondary source of information about them less successful.

The popularity of microcomputers has led to the availability of software suitable for training staff and users, particularly in acquiring skills in online work: here again information on availability is unreliable.

Returning to the literature as a whole, it is apparent that the UK and North America are the sources for a great proportion of it. This is not merely because we prefer to read only what is written in English and to ignore the rest, but in fact the library and information world tends to use English as its international language. India, Scandinavia, South Africa, Australia and New Zealand are rich sources, and use English naturally or by custom for international communication. The growth of literature in Japanese has been well tracked by *Informatics Abstracts*, which we shall examine in Chapter 6; this service also thoroughly surveys the Eastern European literature. *Library and Information Science Abstracts* is also exploring coverage of Japanese output. The professional literature in China is also now beginning to grow – journals are discussed by Meng-Fen Su (1984).

There is little literature originating from continental Europe and the sources we shall describe cover it adequately. The standard French professional literature has been recently surveyed by M. Wagner-Urbain (1984). German and Austrian material is tracked by *Nachrichten für Dokumentation*, mentioned in Chapter 6.

Indian material is prolific and has been described by Umapathy (1981) and more recently by the present author and M.P. Satija (1986). *Library and Information Science Abstracts* has made particular efforts to cover the expanding literature from the developing countries.

Whatever its merits, there has been a lack of interest in non-English language material; a news item in the *Library Association Record* in 1979 reported that one of the largest foreign language collections, at the College of Librarianship Wales, had received no requests for translations from outside the College, despite the wide circulation of *SPEL*, their foreign language current awareness service (Library Association, 1979). This minimal interest provokes no action in acquisition or exploitation, and a letter in reply to the article decries even the attempt (McElroy, 1979).

As 'soft sciences', librarianship and information science suffer in any event in multi-language indexing; Anthony Thompson produced a *Vocabularium Bibliothecarii* for Unesco in 1953, and with more languages in 1963, and a supplement was published by FID in 1964, but nothing more has been seen, although Unesco intend at some time to produce a vocabulary of documentation (Thompson, 1975). Further to aid machine indexing an *Intermediate Lexicon* was assembled as a neutral switching language for information science; this was an experimental version only, the field being selected as 'fraught with terminological ambiguity and difficulty of concept structure', and therefore likely to exhibit all of the problems that the literature of any other subject field might present (Coates, 1970).

4   A strategy for searching

In the subsequent chapters we shall be discussing the principal services in librarianship and information science that lead the researcher onwards to primary sources and suggestions of other routes and different approaches. In beginning a search, the reader probably has a fairly clear idea of what sort of topic the search is about; but we of all professions should realize that our own private and idiosyncratic understanding of our own topic may well differ from someone else's view of that same topic, in scope or delimitation or historical perspective or professional attitude or in terminology, and that any service of indexing or abstracting will be framed in a set manner using constant terms, which may not be those familiar to the researcher. We must therefore begin a search with a clear definition of our topic – we must do our own reference interview – and then we must frame our topic in a series of terms, maybe with alternatives, which we can compare with the terms cited in whichever service we use.

When we have done this, and it may need several attempts and constant revision in the light of our experience in searching, we must then look at the most general sources for a starting point. One good recent book on the sought topic will give basic information, establish terminology and by means of references will lead to further sources. Parallel to this approach, encyclopedias could be consulted; particularly of course in our field one should turn immediately to *ELIS*, which opens the following chapter. Through the articles themselves, and the references cited, basic information and further reading will be discovered.

A rational next step is to search for bibliographies that should lead to complete files of information. Nowadays such an approach is probably not valid: the impossibility of a published bibliography keeping up with the colossal rate of the appearances of new material is clear if we look at the periods covered by even the most recent bibliographies. While the list is being printed any number of vital articles or reports or theses may appear. So the published bibliography has a role only as a check of historical completeness; depending on the currency of the topic that could be all that is required, but our definition of our profession implies that it is not a static affair.

Having established a basic ground, the researcher will then need to use one at least, and preferably as many as feasible, of the abstracting and indexing services discussed in the next chapter. These will facilitate an updating of older information and a complete review of recent serial articles, theses, and reports. This depth of search is generally sufficient for most purposes; but the writer of a thesis, for example, may want all possible information regardless of whether it is published or not. For this also the sources we have indicated above and those which are discussed later will reveal where are the 'centres of excellence' in a particular topic which could be approached for advice, and the authors of key papers could themselves be contacted for a latest view. Obviously their reaction will depend on the importance of the enquiry, and the degree of effort that the researcher has put into investigating through the literature.

Accessibility of cited materials is not generally a problem; the availability of serials is good – the British Library Document Supply Centre will supply to any country, and many remote libraries even in developed countries find it faster and more efficient to send there than to their own national or professional association collections. In North America many fine and comprehensive collections of professional literature can be found. Report literature is accessible through similar sources, or through national clearinghouses. Translations from foreign languages, especially the less common, can be awkward or expensive to obtain; once again national libraries and professional associations are the first contacts to make. Access is not the primary concern of this book, and should give the professional researcher in the Western world little trouble, provided care is taken to transcribe references accurately and quote sources: all this is after all the essence of our business.

We shall still assume that initially the searcher will concentrate on printed sources; when a clear picture of the topic has been obtained and the list of productive terms has been finalized after using the printed versions, then it might be appropriate to use online versions. This will depend on the depth and extent of the search, and the resources available. At an elementary level, printed sources will allow the searcher to browse for related subjects and see the citation in a context of related items, and will reduce the risk of overlooking a vital search term. The special attention that a user embarking on an online search receives is of course equally valuable with printed sources, helping to define the topic, narrow the terms, set parameters and choose the most appropriate sources. Champlin (1985), in recommending such an approach, urges that the printed source may be cheaper, simpler and better at many levels. The expertise gained will in any case be relevant also to the source online, or via CD-ROM, and lead to a better, more productive result.

5 · Major sources of information: Encyclopedic sources

As we have discussed, information changes rapidly; the time that passes between the initial researching of a book, its writing, correcting, printing and final publication can be two years or more, and will normally be in the region of eight to fifteen months. The author may well be using notes and information several months or years old at the time of writing, and consequently currency of information presented in book form will be poor. Nonetheless, the textbook at present forms the basic foundation for students in most disciplines. The information we gain from books has to be seen in a historical context: for any subject, however slow-moving, recent developments will be found in more immediate sources – periodicals, annual reports and research projects, and Chapter 6 will discuss the means of investigating these.

For the purposes of gathering preliminary information about a topic within our subject fields, textbooks and other monograph publications are a starting point, but nothing more. They record the situation as it was at the time of writing, and therefore an enormous amount of sound information can be accumulated. But we must bear in mind the purposes of a search: almost certainly a project or enquiry will not specify that the information should be two years out of date, or rely on someone else's data-collecting ability. Monographs can therefore be used to provide the background information; we should read the relevant chapters of a book to find out the general picture, then supplement it with more recent material. Use a book also for the historical research that it contains: the bibliographical notes in a good textbook will record all the useful articles and monographs in that field for many years past, and provided the book is a standard accepted text the bibliographies should be reliable. This obviously cuts out the necessity of retrospective searching over several years, although this will still be essential if a full-scale research project is being undertaken, to ensure completeness, or if the area being researched has not been covered by a recent monograph. For British material a useful survey of professional literature is available (Ollé, 1981).

Together with textbooks, encyclopedias provide the same type of preliminary background. The same fundamental problems persist: the information recorded is correct some months before publication, and editions of encyclopedias will remain in use over several years, but provided these limitations are accepted, the basic information provides the starting point.

There is one major work in our fields, which, although faulty in many respects, nevertheless is an amazing achievement of perseverance: it is the *Encyclopedia of Library and Information Science*, edited by Allen Kent, Harold Lancour and Jay E. Daily, (M. Dekker, New York, 1968 to date). This encyclopedia (*ELIS*) was announced as an eighteen-volume set; so far 41 volumes have appeared, and more are expected. Volumes 34 and 35 were index volumes to the main 33-volume set; subsequent volumes have been issued as supplements.

The work is certainly authoritative; the opening pages of each volume list the members of the Advisory Board, which has included Sir Frank Francis, Preben Kirkegaard, and Ranganathan. 'The contributors and advisors, however, tend to be yesterday's generation of librarians, many of whom are now retired or dead. Seldom is a fresh or youthful voice heard in *ELIS*', observes Kenneth Kister in a *Library Journal* review (Kister, 1981).

A further review appeared in *Wilson Library Bulletin* featuring a hostile criticism, and a reply from Allen Kent; points made by these reviewers are included in this discussion (Rosenberg and Detlefson, 1973; Kent, 1973).

The preface promises that the 'approach has been strongly international, as expressed through the composition of the Advisory Board, the choice of contributors, and in the editors' instructions to the contributors.'

'A more accurate description of the basic editorial policy would be that this work is not so much inter-national as it is non-national, although, admittedly, this has not been easy to accomplish. Nor, indeed, have we been completely successful in conveying this highly sophisticated notion to all contributors equally. But it has been a constant aim.' (Vol. 1, p. xii)

Obviously the editors are aware of one of their failings: that the articles relating to similar themes in various countries show no standardization of treatment or length.

The preface continues: 'the emphasis has been, throughout, on depth of treatment. While the contributors were urged to stress basic information, they were likewise encouraged to express their evaluative opinions as well and, whenever possible, to suggest and indicate future trends as they saw them.' Here too there is a problem, and many articles adopt a propaganda approach, particularly, as Kister notes, articles on corporate entities – professional associations, library schools, individual libraries and the like: 'the result is not only overly rosy or self-congratulatory profiles but also mighty dull reading.'

The preface, however, does not tell us what we really want to know: there is no definition of the scope, no indication of who is expected to use the information, no indication of the criteria for selecting topics and inviting contributions, and no statement of what editorial control has been exercised.

The chief difficulties therefore that the researcher faces in using *ELIS* are as follows:-

1   The information is out of date; clearly the articles in the early volumes are now twenty years old, and in some areas, like automation and networking, the world has completely changed. Some kind of revision must be maintained or the whole work will rapidly become useless.

2   There is no standardization of approach revealed in depth of treatment, length of articles, or terminology; even a cursory glance in any volume will reveal this. There are two full-scale illustrated articles in volumes 1 and 2 headed 'Architecture, library buildings' and 'Buildings, library'. There is a $7\frac{1}{2}$-page article headed 'Africa, libraries in', but no similar entry for 'Europe' and that for 'Asia' is an expanded cross-reference. Kenya is represented separately under 'Kenya, libraries in', while Nigeria appears only under 'Nigeria, academic libraries in'. Austria is represented only by an article on the national library.

While nine pages are devoted to 'bulletin boards', only 6 go to the 'Bodleian Library', with a further 3 on 'Thomas Bodley'. 'Cambridge University Library', however, is treated in 20 pages.

Given a comprehensive article of over fifty pages on 'Catalogs and cataloging', is it necessary to have a brief separate effort of 5 pages on 'Author catalogs'? Why does the *British National Bibliography* receive only 2½ pages, while *British Technology Index* receives 13? Why does 'Liverpool Polytechnic Library School' merit 23 pages, while other British schools receive no mention (although others are now emerging in the supplements)?

3 The alphabetical arrangement, unless carefully supplemented by use of the index, leads to many problems: Kister observes that 'a major treatment of maps and atlases is part of the article "nonprint material". Because there are currently few cross-references ..., this information is practically inaccessible'.

Even in more recent volumes, for example volume 31, the same problems are still manifest; 'Tunisia, libraries in' receives eleven pages, while 'Toronto University Library' receives 84, and 'Tulane University Library' 52. There is an article headed 'USSR printing', although volume 26 contained an article 'Russia – USSR book printing and libraries'. 'Undergraduate libraries' consume 12 pages, but 'Union activities in US libraries' covers 64. There is a 48-page article on the 'Ukraine, libraries' although nothing appeared on 'Georgia' or 'Lithuania'.

The index volumes (34 and 35) were published in 1983; volume 34 contains an author index, containing citations of contributors' entries, and a referenced author index – this contains entries for personal or corporate authors prominently cited in the text or included in lists of references. In both these indexes all names are indexed as given; no effort has been made to standardize names, so that the same individual may appear separately under entries by surname and initials, or surname and various expanded first names.

The second portion of volume 34 and the whole of volume 35 contain the subject index; the sequence A–F being in volume 34, and

G–Z in volume 35. The index is clearly formatted and is simple to use; it contains both subject and title entries, the latter being in bold type. Acronyms and initialisms are included, as well as *see* and *see also* references, which are especially useful for following corporate name changes. A valuable feature is that new terms are indexed which have come into use during the period of the encyclopedia's currency, so that we are not dependent on the outdated vocabulary of the main work. Generally entries consist of a main term and one subdivision, without any further sub-arrangement; geographical entries are frequent.

Few terms are inverted, and it is necessary to use the index with care to ensure that terms are not overlooked and that we are not confused by US/UK terminology and spelling. One limiting factor, introduced to keep the index to a compact size, is that 'insignificant entries' are not made; if an article is less than one page in length, only the title is indexed. In principle one would expect an index to be fully inclusive of all material, and whether this limitation is in practice inadequate cannot readily be determined: it is certainly suspect.

Since *ELIS* has taken so long to produce, some updating scheme was clearly essential; the method chosen has been to issue supplementary volumes to retain the currency of major articles and provide material on new key areas of activity. The preface to the first supplement (volume 36) notes that 'some articles desperately need updating . . . new topics were unknown twenty years ago', the passage of time makes biographies of deceased personalities necessary, and the original alphabetical arrangement 'forced the omission of material when authors were hopelessly delinquent'.

Each volume is a separate alphabet with a clear table of contents; without scanning the table for each volume the information contained can be traced through the services described in the following chapter, and presumably after a period a supplementary index, or a revised main subject index, will be issued to include the articles in the supplements.

So far six supplements have appeared, and a seventh (volume 42) has been announced for 1987; there are many geographical articles updated, some basic omissions rectified, but still some odd and totally unexpected material – for example 'Horsemanship: its literature and bibliography' (volume 38)!

Despite its faults, *ELIS* is a tremendous achievement; it allows the researcher access to a collected store of information that in most cases is thoroughly authoritative. Even an encyclopedia with faults is better than no encyclopedia at all, and whilst the flaws are considerable, so also is the editors' achievement. Therefore *ELIS* is a good starting point: consult it for essential preliminary information.

In particular, use *ELIS* for its bibliographies. Nearly every article is followed by a good bibliography up to date at the time of compilation, and therefore still very valuable for the later volumes of the set. There appears to be no editorial standardization here either, since some essential topics are followed by a handful of items, while 'Erotica' gets 5½ pages, and 'Union activities in US libraries' receives ten. A bibliography appended to an article in *ELIS* is as valuable as any appearing in a monograph, and the effort put into their compilation should be gratefully adopted by the researcher.

There is only one other encyclopedic source in the English language offering current information, and this is on a completely different scale from *ELIS*. The *ALA World Encyclopedia of Library and Information Services*, edited by Robert Wedgeworth, second edition published in 1986 by the American Library Association and in the UK by Adamantine Press, provides in its 900 pages an important single-volume survey of our field. The *Encyclopedia* was conceived as a companion volume to the *ALA Yearbook*, but has grown into something rather more than this implies. The preface sets out its aim: it seeks to 'explain fundamental ideas, record historical events and activities, and portray those personalities, living and dead, who have shaped the field'.

Unlike *ELIS*, the *World Encyclopedia* has a clearly defined editorial plan, and it is worthwhile to follow its exposition in the preface: firstly there is a series of structured articles on the status and condition of libraries in over 150 countries, and on the history and role of libraries; secondly there are eight articles treating the institutions that provide library and information services, showing the 'purpose, characteristic services, clientele, and patterns of government, finance and administration' in order to demonstrate comparatively the similarities and differences of such bodies in various countries; thirdly there are thirty articles expanding the principles and practices of librarianship and information management. Aside from these categories are articles covering professional education and research, the activities of the more important international agencies and associations, and 218 biographical subjects; these last articles, mostly brief – half to one and a half pages, always with an illustration – cover names of all periods and of many countries, and are selected for their leadership in the profession, for key writings, founding of important libraries, or similar grounds.

The overall result is a series of substantial, authoritative essays which form a first-rate introduction to various aspects of the field. Articles are well laid out, using headings in heavy type to a standard format – for example articles on types of libraries have subsections on 'legislation', 'co-operation', 'acquisition policies' – which makes the scanning of lengthier contributions easier, and editorial control shows its value in the articles on services in a specific country where a concise and even treatment on a similar pattern is a distinct advantage.

Recent developments are suitably represented; there are articles on audio-visual services, on circulation systems, collection development, bilingual and ethnic group services, bibliographic networks, and online information, but not for example on compact disks.

Authorship is worldwide, although inevitably there is a US preponderance, which would be understandable for reasons of time alone. There is little bias detectable, although some articles, for example 'academic libraries', seem to lean too heavily on US examples. The biographees are perhaps more suspect; there are about 120 of US origin, while Europe altogether receives about a third of this number, Africa five, and Asia fifteen.

As a tool for the ready finding of information the *Encyclopedia* has some drawbacks; bibliographically there is not much help. Articles are typically equipped with two or three references, generally to monograph sources; a few have longer bibliographies than this, but many have none at all. The arrangement of the work is interesting: an outline of the whole field to be covered was constructed to allow the greatest cohesion and the minimum of duplication, and this outline now appears in the *Encyclopedia* as the contents table. It proves that much thought and ingenuity has been applied to the conceptual background of the profession and its historical perspective, and it makes a fascinating study in itself, whether or not one ultimately agrees with it. It is not simple to turn to the contents page and look up what one is seeking, it needs some consideration and patience.

However, perhaps the contents list is irrelevant, since the researcher will consult the work by its alphabetical arrangement and by its index. In the first edition a parallel index in the margins was used, and seemed ingenious but not always helpful. In this second edition, a conventional index has been incorporated; it is extensive – some 25 pages, well laid out with clear subheadings and abundant cross references, and it notes illustrations or photographs.

The only other single volume English-language encyclopedia still likely to be commonly found (T. Landau: *Encyclopedia of Librarianship*, 3rd ed., Bowes & Bowes, 1966) is valuable for certain historical points, but in most respects now hopelessly out of date. For simple definitions and summaries it is useful to remember the *Librarian's Glossary and Reference Book* discussed more fully in Chapter 2.

For the British scene, L. J. Taylor's *Librarians' Handbook* (Vol. 1, Library Association, 1976; Vol. 2, Library Association, 1980) presents a formidable quantity of information. The aim was to present policies, statistics, standards and recommendations, found in all manner of sundry documents, together in one volume. The fact that much valuable material appeared in elusive and inaccessible reports, in various versions – draft and final, revised and superseded – or summarized in different periodicals, spurred Taylor to produce a tool well worthy of its name. The first volume begins with central government documents; the introduction to this section comprises a masterly statement of the control exercised by government on libraries of all types, and the channels whereby that control is exercised. The documents, quoted in their full text, include all the public library standards and legislation, the British Library Act and the consultative papers that preceded it, Department of Education and Science circulars relevant to library services, documents from the Library Advisory Council (now the Library and Information Services Council), the Copyright Act and much more.

The following section provides the full texts of all current Library Association policy documents and standards. As well as papers relating directly to libraries by type, the Association has much to say among other things on staffing, reading, bibliographical standards, public lending right, services to handicapped users. The next section performs the same service for other professional bodies; IFLA, Unesco, ARLIS and the Special Libraries Association are represented here.

Other parts of the work cover professional aids; these include all regulations and guides to services produced by the British Library, information on Cataloging in Publication, International Standard Serial Numbering, the Library Licence, the Net Book Agreement, regulations from the Ordnance Survey, VAT provision related to books and libraries, as well as the Library Association documents which comprise the path to the charter. All these are given in full, the complete text of each document.

Statistics are given, drawn from all manner of sources, and including not only library services, but books, publishing, prices and inter-library lending. A directory section lists library book suppliers, equipment suppliers arranged by type of equipment as well as names of firms, contractors for mobile libraries and prefabricated buildings. Smaller areas of the directory cover other services no less essential.

The final part is a bibliographical compendium of the items cited in the volume; the bibliographies vary in their interest – some are superfluous since they have been the subject of previous sections, but others, notably the statistical publications, are most usefully scanned in one short section. This section includes mention of all British Standards in documentation and the equivalent documents of the International Standards Organisation. There is a thorough index, as is obviously essential in a volume of some 850 pages. As if Taylor had not performed a sufficiently remarkable service in preparing the *Handbook*, he went on to compile a second volume which appeared in 1980, and ran to another 1,000 pages. As well as supplementing and updating the first volume, the second accurately reflected the changing face of librarianship and information science by devoting considerable space to databases and networking; documents from BLAISE, Euronet Diane, Prestel, UNISIST, and NATIS are given here.

Statements quoted include Library Association papers on the 'over-production' of librarians, documents from the Civil Service Commission, Voluntary Service Overseas and NATO on the staffing of libraries. Trade union documents on staff in various libraries are included, and the coverage is not only from the UK: statements from the American Library Association appear here also, as they do in the section devoted to 'Obscenity, Censorship, Intellectual Freedom, and the Right to Privacy'. The directory sections of the first volume are expanded, and the whole remarkable pair of volumes concludes with an index of 103 closely-set pages which covers the contents of *both* volumes. These volumes are outstanding, and it is only the passage of time that detracts from their usefulness: the quantity of paper since 1980 has perhaps outgrown this convenient format.

Having consulted encyclopedic sources, and in particular noted items from their bibliographies, the researcher will next need to supplement this information by searching for further bibliographical guides, which, although inevitably behind the times as the previous sources have been, will enable a picture to be built up of the state of the art in the sought topic up until the year or so preceding their publication date.

Here it is necessary firstly to turn to the standard bibliographical sources such as *British National Bibliography* and *Cumulative Book Index* to establish what monograph material has appeared on the relevant subject in recent years. This information for an earlier period can be reliably found through the published catalogue of the Columbia University School (*Dictionary Catalog of the Library of the School of Library Service, Columbia University*, G.K. Hall, Boston, 1962, 7 vols. Supplement, 1976, 4 vols.). This is the largest published bibliographic source in our area and virtually renders redundant the use of other monographic sources for the period of its coverage. A second supplement is in progress, but its likely issue date is unknown. Since 1981 the School's library catalogue has been available on the RLIN database.

Further valuable published guides include *ABHA: annual bibliography of the history of the printed book and libraries* (Nijhoff, The Hague, 1970–) and Theodore Besterman's *Bibliography: library science and reference books: a bibliography of bibliographies* (Rowman and Littlefield, Totowa, NJ, 1971).

More specifically the vast and somewhat dated bulk of retrospective literature is traceable through *Library and information science: a guide to information sources* by D.B. Lilley and R.M. Badough (Gale, Detroit, 1982) which is emphatically American in approach, and *Reference sources in library and information services: a guide to the literature* by G.R. Purcell and G.A. Schlachter (ABC-Clio, Santa Barbara and Oxford, 1984), an exhaustive work including an enormous quantity of material, much of which is inevitably only of historical value.

Obviously there are dozens of published bibliographies relating to libraries, librarianship and information work, and it would be of no assistance to list these again when this task has already been thoroughly done: the reader should spend a little time browsing through a work such as the *Guide to Reference Books* compiled by Eugene Sheehy (9th ed., ALA, Chicago, 1976), its supplements (ALA, Chicago, 1980 and 1982) and tenth edition (1987). The opening sections 'AA' and 'AB' cover general bibliography and our subject areas, running to 96 pages in the main volume and a further 20 in each supplement. By scanning these pages the reader will discover that most aspects of librarianship and information science have been the subject of a bibliography sufficiently recently to be of practical value.

Most of the titles with which a search should start are described by Sheehy; specialized bibliographical guides may list further titles of value. *The International Bibliography of the Book Trade and Librarianship* (12th ed., K.G. Saur, 1981) is especially valuable for countries less well represented in the main stream of literature. Coverage of the UK and USA, although lengthy, is not reliably comprehensive, and the layout of the volumes, using a single typeface for headings, authors, titles and publication details, renders the work frustrating and tiring to consult. Nevertheless much elusive material is included, and particularly for research into comparative librarianship these volumes should not be overlooked. The twelfth edition covers the years 1976–1979 and needs to be supplemented by the tenth and eleventh editions covering respectively 1969–1973 and 1973–1975.

Although it would serve no purpose to itemize bibliographies, it will be useful to consider the pattern of publishing that the researcher might expect to find; the commercial return on the publication of a bibliography is always a poor risk, and in our fields where the potential market is limited most work is published not by commercial publishers but by professional associations and library authorities. This system does have the advantage that tracing of bibliographies need not be an endless task, but can be accomplished by scanning the publications list of professional associations of the country concerned. In Great Britain the Library Association and its various branches and groups have published relevant material, and Aslib has issued several very useful items.

Internationally, IFLA publications, including those of the International Office for UBC, are listed in the *IFLA Directory*, and

FIGURE 5.1

Prefatory Note

BIBLIOGRAPHIC INDEX is a subject list of bibliographies published separately or appearing as parts of books, pamphlets, and periodicals. Selection is made from bibliographies which have fifty or more citations. The Index concentrates on titles in the Germanic and Romance languages. For material in the East European languages the reader is referred to the *Bibliographische Berichte* edited by Staatsbibliothek Preussischer Kulturbesitz and published by Klostermann.

For those unfamiliar with form of reference used in the entries, the following explanation is given:

SAMPLE ENTRY:
Books and pamphlets

Speech, Disorders of
Speech disorders in adults; recent advances; edited by Janis M. Costello. College-Hill Press 1985 incl bibl

Explanation

Several bibliographies on disorders of speech will be found in the book entitled Speech Disorders in Adults; Recent Advances, edited by Janis M. Costello, published by College-Hill Press, in 1985. The full form of the publisher's name and address will be found in the Directory of Publishers and Distributors in Cumulative Book Index.

Camus, Albert, 1913-1960

By and about

Tarrow, Susan. Exile from the kingdom; a political re-reading

...redings of Albert Camus, by Susan Tarrow, published by the University of Alabama Press, in 1985, on pages 208-214. The full form of the publisher's name and address will be found in the Directory of Publishers and Distributors in Cumulative Book Index.

SAMPLE ENTRY:

Periodical articles
Explanation

Commercial law

Recent literature. See issues of Business Lawyer annot

An annotated bibliography on commercial law entitled Recent Literature will be found in every issue of Business Lawyer.

Human information processing

Johnson, E. J. and Payne, J. W. Effort and accuracy in choice. Manage Sci 31:412-14 Ap '85

A bibliography on human information processing entitled Effort and Accuracy in Choice, by E. J. Johnson and J. W. Payne, will be found in Management Science, volume 31, pages 412-414, the April 1985 issue.

Cross-References

Please note that "see" references made from variant forms of subject headings to the form used in *Bibliographic Index* appear in every issue.

"See also" references made from a subject to related subjects under which additional material may be found appear only in the annual volume. Please consult previous volumes for lists of "see also" references.

BIBLIOGRAPHIC INDEX (ISSN 0006-1255) is published April, August, and with a bound cumulation each December. Sold only on the service basis; apply to publisher for rates. Copyright © 1986 by The H.W. Wilson Company, 950 University Avenue, Bronx, N.Y. 10452. All rights reserved. No part of this work may be reproduced or copied in any form or by any means, including but not restricted to graphic, electronic, or mechanical for example, photocopying, recording, taping, or information and retrieval systems — without the express written permission of the Publisher. Printed in U.S.A.

FIGURE 5.2

Libraries and readers
See also
Libraries and foreign population
Libraries and the aged
Library orientation
Educating the public library user, compiled and edited by John Lubans, Jr. American Lib. Assn. 1983 p138-42

Libraries and schools
See also
Children—Books and reading
Children's literature
School libraries

Libraries and state
See also
Information services and state
United States
Mason, Marilyn Gell. The federal role in library and information services. Knowledge Industry Publs. 1983 p167-72

Libraries and students
See also
Library orientation

Libraries and television
Akroyd, R G. Selected readings on cable, telecommunications and video technologies. (In Cable for information delivery; a guide for librarians, educators and cable professionals; edited by Brigitte L. Kenney. Knowledge Ind. Publs. 1984 p147-63)

Libraries and the aged
See also
Public libraries—Services to the aged
Casey, Genevieve M. Library services for the aging. Library Professional Publs. 1984 incl bibl annot

Libraries and the handicapped
Dequin, Henry C. Librarians serving disabled children and young people. Libraries Unlimited 1983 p255-94
Needham, William L, and Jahoda, Gerald. Improving

Developing countries
Education and training in developed and developing countries; with particular attention to the Asian region. (FID publ, 625) Fédération Int. de Documentation 1983 incl bibl

Library education (Continuing education)
Michaels, Carolyn Leopold. Library literacy means lifelong learning. Scarecrow Press 1985 p341-50

Library employees
See also
Librarians

Library exhibits
See also
Bibliographical exhibitions

Library extension
See also
Libraries and foreign population

Library finance
Trumpeter, Margo C., and Rounds, Richard S. Basic budgeting practices for librarians. American Lib. Assn. 1985 incl bibl

Library information networks
Rao, Dittakavi Nagasankara. Library networks; a selected bibliography. (Public administration series; bibliography P-1596) Vance Bibls. 1984 14p

Library instruction See Library orientation

Library legislation
See also
Libraries and state

Library materials

Library materials Conservation and restoration
Kyle, Hedi. Library materials preservation manual; practical methods for preserving books, pamphlets, and other printed materials; with contributions by Nelly Balloffet [et al]. Smith, N.Y. 1983 p149-56 annot
Morrow, Carolyn Clark, and Walker, Gay. The preservation challenge; a guide to conserving library materials. Knowledge Industry Publs. 1983 p217-25

FID has produced *FID Publications: an eighty-year bibliography 1895–1975* (FID Publication 531, 1975).

To bring up to date the items culled from such bibliographical sources as those we have mentioned, a final part of the search at this stage should concentrate on recently published bibliographies. The best single source for this is *Bibliographic Index*, published by H.W. Wilson and appearing in hard copy three times a year, the last part being a case-bound annual cumulation, which can also be searched online via WILSONLINE. This records bibliographies found in all of the 2,600 or more periodicals that the H.W. Wilson company scan for their other indexes, with the addition of bibliographies in books, and those published separately. The coverage is international and up to date, and the only restriction is that a bibliography must contain at least 50 items to be included – this may exclude valuable material recorded as references to periodical articles, but although regrettable it is obviously realistic.

The page headed *prefatory note*, which begins each issue (Figure 5.1), gives a succinct explanation of the form of entry for books and for periodicals. Items on librarianship and information science are well represented; topics are divided into subheadings, and many sections are expanded by *see also* references. The specimen page reproduced here (Figure 5.2) illustrates the range of coverage, the cross-referencing, and the useful inclusion of standing information on regular sources – the second column of the page shown lists a number of periodicals and abstracts which should be consulted because they regularly publish bibliographies.

The final type of monograph literature to be covered in this chapter is the *Festschrift*; the habit of collecting essays into volumes in commemoration of a person or an event is a successful means of concealing them in library catalogues, unless analytical cataloguing is carried out. Although the abstracting services to be discussed in the next chapter cover most *Festschriften*, the best source to check is J.P. Danton's *Index to Festschriften in Librarianship* (Bowker, 1970) which had an international coverage, and examined items published between the 1860s and 1966. J.P. Danton and J.F. Pulis extended this coverage in a further volume for the years 1967–1975 (K.G. Saur, 1979).

We have attempted in this chapter to consider the information presented in published books, and the problems associated with it. We have been particularly concerned to extract bibliographical citations to allow us to build up a picture of a topic, but there is an inevitable gap, which may be several years, between the compilation date of a book and the present day. To complete our coverage, we must next look at periodicals and the means of accessing them.

6   Major sources of information: Abstracting and indexing services

So far we have considered only information published in monographs and reference works. The second category of publishing is the journal; as already discussed there are several hundred journals directly relevant to our subject fields, and hundreds more in fringe fields.

Clearly the journal is of enormous value; many topics do not lend themselves to monograph publishing because the amount that can be written about them is inadequate for a book, and the potential readership is too limited. The advantages of the journal article, by comparison, are its more concise scale, the improved chance of its being read by subscribers to the journal, and most important of all its currency. Whereas information in a monograph may be years out of date at the time of publication, a journal article can appear within weeks of writing, and even allowing for the most elaborate refereeing methods should appear in print within one year of its compilation. Journals are therefore among the best sources of new information, and of detailed information on specific topics. As we saw in Chapter 3 the number of journals relevant to our subject field may be over 1,500 titles.

The means whereby the whole field of journal publishing can be kept under review are inevitably difficult to envisage. Given the large number of titles, the international origins, and the limited resources available for compilation and publication, the services which this chapter reviews are remarkably helpful. It has to be remembered that, in addition to the journal articles, the services to be described also attempt to keep track of other types of publication – monographs, reports and research papers – and that the journals themselves contain not only recognizable, discreet articles, but a host of reviews, notes, news items and miscellaneous snippets of information which some of the services try to record.

It is unfortunate that even in such a small field as ours several services exist; looking at the whole field of knowledge, the UNISIST feasibility study observed that 'abstract journals now number several thousand. It is sometimes contended that their growth is just as fast as that of the primary journals which they are intended to cover ... [whatever view we take of them] the general lesson seems to be that some form of condensation in natural or stereotyped language is needed, as an intermediate between full text, in which only few scientists have the time, or the competence, to browse productively' (UNISIST, 1971, p.43). The problems of literature growth in our fields have been seen, and although the services we shall consider have not multiplied at the alarming rate suggested by UNISIST we shall nonetheless have to review many services in this chapter alone, and others subsequently, to obtain the basic level of general information. To explore the relevant areas of impinging fields could need even more sources. Despite this, evidence suggests that 'one must use five or six separate services in order to locate 85–90 per cent of the relevant library and information science literature, and second, that 10 to 15 per cent of the literature is not covered by any service' (Tegler, 1979). Current figures will probably be similar (LaBorie, Halperin and White, 1985).

It is important to come to grips with the principal services. For any literature search in librarianship or information science the first two services at least that we shall describe need to be scanned; we need to be aware how the services are arranged, what fields, countries and journals they particularly cover, how speedily they appear, what their indexing arrangements are, and who their compilers are.

We shall begin with a British service – *Library and Information Science Abstracts (LISA)*. The Library Association first became involved with an abstracts service in 1950 with the start of *Library Science Abstracts*. This service continued until 1968, and was initially the work of voluntary labour, and editors with full-time jobs putting it together in their spare time. It is a measure of the growth in scale and complexity of the literature in our subject fields that such an approach would now be unthinkable. Over the years full-time professional staff were employed, and at present the whole compilation is handled by staff employed by Library Association Publishing, Ltd, with a small group of outside abstractors used for foreign language material. In 1969 *Library Science Abstracts* changed its format to A4, and its title to *Library and Information Science Abstracts* to reflect its expanded coverage.

In 1976 the coverage of information science was further enhanced by an agreement with Aslib, whose specialist staff would provide abstracts in specific areas. This co-operation lasted until the end of 1980, although some Aslib-compiled abstracts continued to appear in 1981, and all the information science areas are now covered internally. Also in 1976 computerized methods of production were introduced.

Except for historical searches *Library Science Abstracts* is now little consulted. Its arrangement is very simple, and no problems would arise in its use; there are cumulated indexes for the years 1950–1955 and 1956–1960, which will speed up any search. There is then an awkward eight-year gap before the first cumulated index to *LISA*, and it is unlikely now that this hiatus will be mended, as the period covered is of little importance except historically.

The coverage of *LISA* is now extensive; its traditional area of librarianship has been thoroughly covered, information science is now equally strong and there is a good spread over the most frequently sought fringe areas – publishing, bookselling, reprography, as well as electronic publishing, word-processing and videotex. International coverage is good; *LISA* abstracts journals from about 100 countries, and in twenty languages, and the result of this policy has been that 80 per cent of subscribers are outside the UK. Fifty per cent of the journals scanned originate in Western Europe, with a further 25 per cent from North America. Percentages from the rest of the world are – Eastern Europe and the USSR 10 per cent, Asia 8 per cent, Africa 4 per cent, and Australia/New Zealand 3 per cent. *LISA* has made particular efforts to obtain and abstract journals from developing countries, and there are now over 30 such titles, mainly from Commonwealth countries (Moore, 1981). Expansion into Japanese literature is a current priority. There is a bias towards European journals, and given that the other main English-language service – *Library Literature* – is heavily US-orientated, this is no bad thing. In fact, despite the apparently large number of services for such a small area of literature, overlap is small: between 65 per cent and 75 per cent of relevant journals are covered only by one service (LaBorie, Halperin and White, 1985) and therefore for Western European sources *LISA* is the best place to search if restricted to the English language.

Whilst it is good on journals, *LISA* used to be criticized for its

FIGURE 6.1

Rmi—INSTRUCTIO' S IN USE OF LIBRARIES AND LIBRARY MATERIALS (Continued)

'user education', describes the method of user education employed at BCS, and offers an evaluation of the user education programme undertaken. (A.G.)

RmiHypD438—School children. Poland   **86/4627**

O lekcjach bibliotecznych raz jeszcze. [More on library classes.] Irena Borecka *Poradnik Bibliotekarza,* 37 (4) 1985, 111-114, 122.

The Polish Ministry of Education's 1983 syllabuses for the 10-year state school programme envisaged lessons in library use for all pupils throughout their school career. Lack of lesson-time and sometimes inadequate preparation of the programme have often caused difficulties in the implementation of the programme. Gives 3 typical lesson plans for library instruction classes at different levels to cover: use of the library for infants; structure and use of the book; archives and museum as repositories of documents. (Z.G.)

RmiKza—Local history collections. School children. UK. British   **86/4628**
Association for Local History

School local history projects: how BALH is trying to help. David Hayns. *Local Studies Librarian,* 4 (1) Summer 85, 14-17.

Because of a shortage of time teachers are often not able to undertake detailed research and preparation necessary to guide students through project work, and librarians, archivists and museum curators bear the brunt of the work. Describes attempts made by the British Association for Local History (BALH) to help students with project work. These included 2 courses run in Saffron Walden and Leicester, the aim of which was to provide background information and basic techniques to help with project work. Discusses plans for similar courses in Saffron Walden, Matlock and Portsmouth during 1985. (A.G.)

Rmf—BIBLIOGRAPHICAL CONTROL

RmfFsD4373—National libraries. Czechoslovakia. Slovakia.   **86/4629**
Matica Slovenska

Koordinácia bibliografickej činnosti na Slovensku. [Coordination of bibliographic work in Slovakia.] Soňa Budinská. *Čitatel',* 34 (7-8) 268-269. 34 refs.

Rp—SELECTIVE DISSEMINATION OF INFORMATION (SDI)
(Continued)

ments.] V.S. Lazarev. *Nauchnye i Tekhnicheskie Biblioteki SSSR,* (6) 1985, 6-11. 29 refs.

Feedback cards are used to evaluate the relevance of references produced by SDIs. Discusses their utilisation and advises on the type of information which should be recorded on them and, subsequently, evaluated. Shows that while feedback cards are an effective tool for the evaluation of users' requirements they are not suitable for the evaluation of the quality of the SDI profiles. (Z.H.)

Rr/s—ABSTRACTING AND INDEXING SERVICES

Rs—INDEXING SERVICES

RsM(61)—Medicine. Index Medicus   **86/4633**

A brief history of Index Medicus. Susan Symonds. *Current Studies in Librarianship,* 8 (1/2) Spring/Fall 84, 35-38. 12 refs.

Gives a brief history of *Index Medicus.* Discusses its development from the late 1800s, its expanding services and its involvement in on-line technology. (S.E.)

Ru/v—REFERENCE WORK

RuGdEr(7)D73—University libraries. Fine arts libraries. USA   **86/4634**

Remembrance of things past: mental processes of the art reference librarian. Deirdre Corcoran Stam. *Art Documentation,* 4 (4) Winter 85, 139-141. 11 refs.

In 1985 this writer interviewed the heads of 6 university art libraries in the Midwest and Atlantic regions, asking them what mental and physical steps they take to answer patrons' questions. Most accounts of reference work assume that the librarian's problem is finding enough material to answer the question. For art reference librarians the problem appears to be to select from the many possible sources known to them the one which will produce the right information, at the correct level, with the appropriate bias or approach. Both logical search strategy and memory are involved. (E.A.)

RmfLqf—Theses *and* Dissertations   86/4630

Research dissertations: problems of acquisition. L.S. Ramaiah, T.V. Prafulla Chandra. *Herald of Library Science.* 24 (3) July 85, 202-206. 10 refs.

The university library services and collections exist to support the research and learning functions of the university. Considers the need to avoid duplication of research thereby saving effort, time and money, by achieving universal access to research dissertations. Examines attempts at bibliographical control of research dissertations in the USA, UK, West Germany and India. Discusses acquisition problems and suggests prerequisites of a standard mechanism for obtaining research dissertations at both national and international levels which would include provisions for deposit, loan and photocopying. (A.G.)

RmfNbcsD481—Organisation and administration. National policies. Norway   86/4631

En samkatalog, en MARC-brønn og en nasjonalbibliografi. [A union catalogue, a MARC store and a national bibliography.] Hans Martin Fagerli. *Bok og Bibliotek.* 52 (6) 1985, 279-281. illus.

The Evaluation Project (1977-79) saw a central model as the only realistic solution to the problems of a national integrated bibliographic system. But since the project, developments have largely gone against it, with many libraries installing their own data systems. Outlines an alternative model taking account of this fact. It describes a national library system consisting of a network to which the common resources: the union catalogues for books and periodicals, the MARC store, UBO-BOK, and other data bases are connected. The libraries outside the network must communicate by telephone. Summarises the aims of the individual parts: the separate library systems must ensure that they can deliver data to the catalogues, which must simplify their bibliographic content and be a system for location and inter-lending only; the UBO-BOK (the national bibliographies) must include more categories of Norwegian material and the MARC store must be developed to include the most common national MARC services. A common MARC store will supply the Union catalogues and the different library systems with machine readable data. Outlines the organisational, technical, economic and employment consequences of this decentralised model. (E.L.D.)

Rn/1—INFORMATION SERVICES (PUBLISHED AND DISTRIBUTED SERVICES)

Rp—SELECTIVE DISSEMINATION OF INFORMATION (SDI)

RpNh—Evaluation. User feedback   86/4632

Karta obratnoi svyazi kak instrument izucheniya informatsionnykh potrebnosti. [Feedback cards as a tool for determination of users' require-

---

Gray Kraft and Anne Engelhart; wearing someone else's shoes: reference in an established archive, by Edward C. Oetting; The past in the present: reference in a British university archival collection, by F.W. Ratcliffe; Archival reference at a technical university, by Elizabeth C. Stewart; Of books, manuscripts and jars of snakes: reference service in the museum, archives and records management section, Toronto Board of Education, by Susan McGrath; Life in the fast lane: reference in a business archives, by Cynthia G. Swank; Researching the past: an archivist's perspective, by Frank A. Zabrosky; The paper chase: reference service in the bank's archives, by Anne Van Camp; The challenge of contemporary records: reference service in a labor and urban archives, by Philip P. Mason; The manuscript that isn't, by Charles Clement; A well-kept secret: the religious archive as reference resource, by Rosalie McQuaide; Reference service in Catholic diocesan archives, by James M. O'Toole; Establishing an image: the role of reference service in a new archival program, by Thomas Wilsted; 'What do you have on Arthur Flegenheimer?' Research and reference at the Franklin D. Roosevelt Library, by Raymond Teichman; Reference and in regional history centers, by Glen A. Gildemeister; Expanded access to archival sources, by Thomas Hickerson. (N.L.M.)

Rx—DOCUMENT DELIVERY

RxKn—Availability of documents. Government publications. Public libraries   86/4636

Available for all to use? Planning documents in public libraries. C.E. Makepeace. *Local Studies Librarian.* 4 (1) Summer 85, 3-9.

Edited version of a paper given at a seminar on information resources for leisure and recreation held on 3 Nov 83, jointly organised by the Library Association (LA) Reference Special and Information Section (RSIS) and Asib. Depsite the bias towards documents which relate to tourism, recreation and leisure, the information provided would apply equally to other planning department documents. These documents are an important source of local information, but they are difficult to locate and not always available in public libraries. Discusses the reasons for and the extent of the shortfall in public libraries, and whether there are any types of material which are not picked up or whether the gaps are in all types of material. After discussing types of material produced by planning departments and associated bodies and types of material available in public libraries, suggests methods for improvement of library coverage. (A.G.)

Ry—CULTURAL ACTIVITIES (EXTENSION WORK)

Ry &—Summer events. Children's libraries. Public libraries   86/4637

Letná aktivita—alebo odpočinok? [Summer activity—or á rest?] Juraj Spiner. *Citateľ.* 34 (7-8) 1985, 291-292.

Discusses the work of the libraries in the summer, with emphasis on the work of libraries located in holiday resorts. Describes the preparation of poor coverage of monographs and reports. This lack has now been rectified, and a large number of monographs and theses (both English-language only) are now included, totalling some 18 per cent of the database. It is worth pointing out that *LISA* specifically does not cover feature articles of less than one page, nor news items, nor minor pieces of information.

Now that we have considered its history, and its present coverage, we need to examine the service that *LISA* provides and the way it is arranged. *LISA* appeared six times a year until the end of 1981; in 1982 a monthly service began. The time-lag between the date of publication of the original item and the date of the appearance of the abstract has always been remarkably good, sometimes as little as two to three months, although there have been occasions when production problems worsened this, and in 1981 the average was between six and nine months. Monthly publication has obviously reduced this.

One of the main features of *LISA* is that a full informative abstract is provided for each item, together with a full bibliographical citation showing the title in the original language, a transliteration if the original is Cyrillic, a translated title if the original is non-English, the author (although no designation is given), then journal title, volume, part, the date including the month, page numbers, and indications of illustrations, tables or references. The sample page (Figure 6.1) shows the style of abstract – generally 120–150 words – and the detailed citation.

There is unease at author-compiled abstracts – because there is no control over bias, and at secondary-source abstracts – because again there is no control over the accuracy or quality provided. Consequently *LISA* has always attempted to compile abstracts in-house, and indicates after each entry the compiler or other source. The abstract is always impartial, and must not be critical or evaluative.

As has been mentioned, *LISA* has used computerized production methods since 1976, and it is available in magnetic tape form, and on CD-ROM, and can be searched online through Derwent-SDC ORBIT and Lockheed DIALOG (File 61). The database from 1969 to the end of 1985 numbered some 74,000 records.

The arrangement of *LISA* is as thorough as its other features, and is consequently a little difficult to understand, and has been the principal cause of criticism of the service. In fact, although to say so reduces the value of the service, *LISA* can be quite satisfactorily used without even appreciating the finer points of its arrangement, provided care is taken to avoid overlooking features which a full search would reveal.

The basis of the arrangement is the 1971 unpublished draft of the *Classification Research Group Scheme for the Classification of Library Science (CRG)*, which employs an alphabetical notation for core subjects and numerical for the fringes, and is a faceted scheme. An outline of the scheme appears inside the rear cover of each issue. Combining facets enables very specific classification numbers to be obtained, but this can result in long and confusing notation – for example Hyk Hu Efp Ex (Hospital patient libraries in the Netherlands) and SheM(78)MvFvD471 (Loans of music in Finnish public libraries), although the great majority of entries are of only one or two facets – for example Sft (Theft detection) or Npk (Fees for Services).

For subject work on a specific topic therefore *LISA* is excellent, with the specific term being accessible directly, or through use of the indexes. However, simple scanning of one place in each issue could overlook scattered items, and foolproof retrieval demands an understanding not only of the basic scheme but of its citation order as well, and a check in the index is probably always advisable except for the experienced user.

For most users, the normal means of approach will be through the indexes; each issue contains a name index and a subject index printed on black-edged paper at the end. These indexes cumulate to form an annual index issue, so that bound sets will typically include only the annual index part and not the single issue indexes as well.

The name index (until 1978 there was only an author index) includes, as well as conventional authors, entries for acronyms, organizations, systems, networks, conferences and symposia, many of which would previously have appeared in a subject index. Thus OCLC, ORBIT and ORACLE, for instance, should be sought in the name index. Additional entries are given under alternative forms of names. Each name index entry is followed by the number of the abstract in the annual volume. Each separate issue contains abstracts

FIGURE 6.2

in a classified order which are assigned a running number, beginning with number 1 each January and continuing through the separate parts to 6,000 or more by December. Each issue index refers to the abstracts within that issue, and at the end of the year the whole file forms a complete sequence. For reference outside the annual volume context, each abstract is normally cited by the abbreviated year and abstract number, thus 86/2179 – abstract no. 2179 in the 1986 annual file.

The alphabetical subject index, which appears and cumulates in the same manner as the name index, is compiled by chain indexing. In some cases entries are rotated to provide a better display, or when an inflexible adherence to the chain procedure would result in meaningless terms.

This method is economical in production, but has the in-built snag that no relationships are shown between terms, so that the user must formulate a search with a variety of alternative terms, and when a number of abstracts have been traced the surrounding abstracts in the classified sequence should also be scanned.

Whereas in the classified sequence of abstracts the primary grouping is by technical processes, in the subject index the only fully specific entry is given under the last term in the classification number. As a result the subject index includes numerous entries for types of libraries, countries and subject areas, but few for technical processes (see, for example, the subject index page, Figure 6.2). The user must therefore search around in the classified sequence, having first identified likely places from the subject index. Since each bound annual volume consists of the twelve monthly parts, the user must carry out this scanning process in each of the original parts, that is, in twelve places within each annual sequence. Obviously to use the service online or on CD-ROM will save an enormous amount of time in a large-scale search.

A particular problem occurs with geographical areas, where, for any given topic, all index entries for the country concerned need to be inspected. This can be time-consuming in the case of major literature-producing countries; for example, for information on computerization in libraries in the USA, almost six columns of small-face type need to be checked in the 1984 annual index. Merely to look at *USA*, then *Computer*, overlooks further entries where the computer facet appeared in a different position in the citation order, for instance *USA. Federal government; publications: computerised cataloguing.*

There are two cumulated index volumes, covering the years 1969–1973 and 1976–1980; the first includes an author index and a subject index. The second cumulation contains the subject and name indexes restructured into a single alphabetical sequence.

It may well be helpful in consolidating the information on *LISA* so far presented to conduct two sample searches to demonstrate the features noted: first of all consider a topic such as *teenage use of public libraries*, and any international comparisons.

There are a variety of approaches; if we look at the entries for *public libraries* in the annual subject index for 1984, we shall find four columns of subordinate terms – rather daunting to scan maybe – and if we look for *teenagers* here we shall find nothing. However, if we look for *teenagers* as a separate term, we find we are referred to *youth*. We can use this term in combination with *public libraries* and find twelve abstract numbers further divided, for instance into *users*, and *microcomputers*. There is no way of combining the international aspect through the index, unless we search under the entries for all relevant countries, an inaccurate and time-consuming business, but if we consult the sequence of abstracts we can browse easily to pick up more items of relevance. One of the abstracts listed is no. 3035: this we find in the numerical sequence, and we discover that we are in a section headed *Ru Hyk/k – Youth and Children's Libraries* under the general heading *Reference work.* If we look at other abstracts at the same classification number and those around it, we see that we have a number of items on similar topics. We may now look at the other eleven monthly sections of the 1984 volume under the same classification number in each section, and search previous years also if required.

If we consider a second search that features routines and materials – for example *cataloguing of audio-visual materials* – we need to remember that the arrangement of the classified sequence is primarily by technical process, and therefore to search the subject index by such a term is fruitless. To look at *cataloguing* therefore leads to no helpful entries, and no references elsewhere. To search under *audio-visual materials*, however, and then *cataloguing* as a subordinate term yields results. Once again we find that the abstracts traced are surrounded by similar topics where it might be valuable to browse, and we have been given a classification number which we can use to search in other separate issues and annual volumes. If we wanted information on the treatment of audio-visual materials by networks, we should also remember that acronymic titles such as *OCLC* will be found in the name index, not the subject index.

If we consider that possible uses of *LISA* include current awareness, preparation of bibliographies, and comparative librarianship searches, then we are very well served; *LISA* is adequately up to date, international in coverage, though with a European bias, comprehensive in its coverage of fringe areas, concise, informative and easy to use – despite the critics of *CRG*.

The other main English-language service is very different in approach and arrangement, and offers a significantly different type of assistance. *Library Literature* is an indexing service, not an abstracting service, so its entries record only the existence of an item, and give no information about its content or coverage,

Library Literature first appeared in 1934, produced by the American Library Association's Junior Members Round Table, and was intended to continue the coverage of H.G.T. Cannon's *Bibliography of Library Economy 1872–1920*, which was published in 1927. The first volume of *Library Literature* covered the years 1921–1932, and after its appearance the H.W. Wilson Company took over production and publication, beginning with the volume 1933–35. From 1936 an annual volume was produced, changing to semi-annual in 1939. From 1955 *Library Literature* appeared quarterly, and from 1969 six issues have appeared each year, followed by a bound annual volume. In 1969 the subtitle was altered to 'an index to library *and information* science'. H.W. Wilson have remained the publishers from 1933, and consequently *Library Literature* has always been viewed as a commercial venture. H.W. Wilson were late into the online world, and access to *Library Literature* via WILSONLINE began only late in 1985. A user-friendly gateway, WILSEARCH, will help inexperienced end users, but skilled users can contact WILSONLINE directly. A CD-ROM service, WILSONDISC, will also contain *Library Literature*.

Library Literature has a wide coverage of journals; about 220 titles are scanned, of which 140 or so are of US origin. Not surprisingly, whether a cause or effect of this statistic, *Library Literature* is used in the States almost to the exclusion of any other service, except in specialized institutions. Coverage of non-English-language titles forms only about 12–15 per cent of the total, and surprisingly there are no Latin American titles represented. In comparison with *LISA*, this service is therefore heavily US-biased, but it does offer other features, which makes its coverage valuable even outside that geographical area; notably it is not selective in indexing, but records journal contents from cover to cover, including all feature articles, regardless of how brief, reviews, news items and notes. Consequently the number of entries is much greater than in *LISA*; the number of unique titles covered only by *Library Literature* is very small, but the depth of coverage yields much more material than other services.

The speed of appearance of an index entry after publication of the original item seems to vary enormously. A glance at any issue will show delays of between three months and a year on US-produced sources, and for non-US sources delays are typically between one and two years. Despite its easier compilation, therefore, with no abstracts to be provided, *Library Literature* is slow in production. Issues do however appear promptly and computerized production may reduce the time-lag. The British user will find problems of terminology; the natural language headings are strictly American, and can cause difficulties to the non-US user, and the vocabulary of the field is in any case soft and unstable. For too many journal articles (for example in *Library Journal*) prefer a catchy title which gives little clue to their contents.

Despite the change in its subtitle to include *information, Library Literature* remains very much more angled to traditional librarianship. To a great extent this is a result of its slow reaction to new journal titles – and it is on the information science side of our subject area that the increase in publishing has been greater – and the substantial volume of entries produced overall, which tends to swamp small and specific areas with multiple-entry coverage of more general information.

Library Literature also includes two separate features of interest; at the end of each issue is a list of book reviews – each item listed is followed by references to places in which a review may be found, and a checklist of monographs cited for the first time – a useful means of keeping track of new publishing. Citations in this section include details of publishers and prices.

FIGURE 6.3

SAMPLE ENTRIES

For those unfamiliar with the form of reference used in the entries, the following explanation is given:

Periodical entry: **Fees for library service**
Rochell, C. C. The knowledge business: economic issues of access to bibliographic information. *Coll Res Libr* 46 5-12 Ja '85; Discussion 46:438 S '85

Explanation: An article on the subject **Fees for library service** by C. C. Rochell entitled "The knowledge business: economic issues of access to bibliographic information" will be found in *College & Research Libraries*, volume 46, pages 5-12 in the January 1985 issue.
Discussion of this article appears in *College & Research Libraries*, volume 46, page 438 in the September 1985 issue.
Full forms of authors' names will be found in the author entry.

Blanket reference: **Instruction in library use**
Woo, C. and Fink, D. BI line: a column on bibliographic instruction See issues of Colorado Libraries

Explanation: A regular feature on the subject of **Instruction in library use** by C. Woo and D. Fink entitled "BI line: a column on bibliographic instruction " appears in each issue of *Colorado Libraries*.

Thesis entry: **Women librarians**
Anatolin, L. K. D. Women in management: a review of the literature of

the University of Chicago for the Master of Arts degree. It contains 247 pages.

Book entry:

Statistics

Public libraries

Denmark Library Inspectorate. Folkebiblioteksstatistik 1985; budgetter 1985; virksomhed 1984 (Public library statistics 1985; budgets 1985; activities 1984). Bibliotekscentralens Forlag 1985 88p charts

Explanation:

A book about **Statistics** of **Public libraries** by the Denmark Library Inspectorate entitled "Folkebiblioteksstatistik 1985; budgetter 1985; virksomhed 1984," the English translation of which is "Public library statistics 1985; budgets 1985; activities 1984," was published by Bibliotekscentralens Forlag in 1985. It contains 88 pages and includes charts.

Full forms of publishers names and addresses will be found in the "Directory of Publishers and Distributors" in *Cumulative Book Index*, or in other international directories and bibliographical sources.

Analytic entry:

Friends of the library

Ruffner, F. G., Jr. Friends of libraries. (*In* The ALA yearbook of library and information services, v10, 1985. American Lib. Assn. 1985 p128-9) il

Explanation:

An article on the subject **Friends of the library** by F. G. Ruffner, Jr. entitled "Friends of libraries" appears in *The ALA yearbook of library and information services* volume 10, 1985. The article appears on pages 128-129 and is illustrated. Full information about the book appears in its main entry.

Book review:

Thomason, N. W. Circulation systems for school library media centers. 1985

SLJ 32.32 Ja '86. J. Roeder

Explanation:

A review of a book by N. W. Thomason entitled "Circulation systems for school library media centers" and published in 1985 will be found in *SLJ*, volume 32, page 32 in the January 1986 issue. The author of the review is J. Roeder.

Library Literature also usefully indexes obituaries, and appoint-ments by the name of the person, and the name of the library or other institutions. A further area where it is unique is its coverage of US library school theses, and the great variety of US state association journals.

The arrangement of *Library Literature* is the conventional dictionary system: a single alphabetical sequence comprises authors, titles, subject headings and cross references. The users' approach is therefore to think of the relevant terms for the search undertaken and simply look them up in the alphabetical sequence. Cross references pass the user from sought terms to preferred terms where necessary, and although these are numerous it is with the cross references that problems are most likely to arise. In many cases items are indexed in two or three places, but terms used are specific, and may conceal secondary subjects, and the cross references cannot adequately cover all possibilites. In addition it should be noted that indexing terms do change over the years, and that a retrospective search cannot reliably be carried out with one set of terms only – all likely terms need to be checked in each volume. Further, cross references are only included in parts where the preferred term has been used; it is therefore essential to check more than one annual volume to discover all possible terms.

Because of terminological difficulties and Americanisms, it is necessary to experiment with a wide range of terms before embarking on a search, to ensure that all relevant information is recovered. Generally, *Library Literature* is easy to use, provided care is taken to isolate the right indexing terms; entries are divided by subheadings, and geographically where appropriate. Each entry includes the author's name (without designation), the title in the original language if non-English, followed by a translation, the title of the monograph or journal (journal titles are abbreviated, and a list appears at the start of each issue). Volume numbers are given (but not the part number) and page numbers and date, including the month. There is no indication of illustrations, references, or bibliographies. The sample introductory page (Figure 6.3) shows the various types of entry and gives a full explanation of each.

To demonstrate the ease of approach, and some of the difficulties, we shall again search for the two topics we sought in *LISA*, using the issue of *Library Literature* for August 1986; the first was *teenage use of public libraries*, with any international comparisons. *Teenagers* is not an index term, neither is *youth*, but in looking for *youth* we should find *young adults' library services*, *young adults' literature* and *young adults' reading* – all subdivided by topic and geographically. To look at the term *public libraries* predictably opens the floodgates to five columns of entries, all of which need scanning to obtain a complete picture, since their subdivisions specify processes and services as well as user groups, and the geographically divided entries account for almost half of the total. The index term *public libraries in schools* could also be of value. To look at the entries for various likely countries produces only references to those subject headings under which those countries appear in the issue we are consulting. Given differences in the educational system between the UK and the US our search ought also to include *school libraries* and *college and university libraries*; again both involve scanning numerous entries.

The second search was concerned with the *cataloguing of audio-visual materials*; here *Library Literature* seems too easy – we can find *audio-visual materials* as an index term, and *cataloguing*. However, there are more relevant entries for example under *films*, and *recordings*, and although it seemed so simple, we need to think of all possible headings and look at them, and even then there is always the doubt that the terminology that the indexer used has eluded us. In all cases of course the entry we find records only the details of author, title and citation; there is no further guidance on the possible relevance to our search that an abstract would give.

Two specimen pages of *Library Literature* are reproduced here; the first (Figure 6.4) demonstrates the use of cross references, and the useful division of large subjects by subheadings, although the general nature of all the terms used on this page may lead to uncertainty. The second (Figure 6.5) shows an example of coverage in the information science field, although as we observed some newer titles are not covered. The difficulties of indexing by general natural language are formidable.

Although *LISA* and *Library Literature* are the best known services, there are several others that should be consulted for complete coverage, and we shall now turn to a briefer consideration of these:

Informatics Abstracts is an English language version of *Referativnyj Zhurnal, Section 59: Informatika* which has been published since 1963 by VINITI – the All-Union Institute of

FIGURE 6.4

Librarianship—Psychological aspects—*cont.*

Anderson. A. J. New librarian in town [with discussion] *Libr J* 110:47-9 O 15 '85

Personality traits of men in female-dominated jobs. *Libr J* 110:32 O 1 '85

Research

See Research in librarianship

Social aspects

See also

Librarians—Social responsibilities

Libraries and social and economic problems

Birdsall. W. F. Community, individualism. and the American public library. *Libr J* 110:21-4 N 1 '85

Michell. B. G. and Harris, R. M. Evaluating the competence of information providers (*In* 1984: challenges to an information society. Knowledge Industry Publs. 1984 p63-7) charts

Nitecki. D. A. Competencies required of public services librarians to use new technologies (*In* Clinic on Library Applications of Data Processing (20th: 1983: University of Illinois at Urbana-Champaign). Professional competencies—technology and the librarian. University of Ill. at Urbana-Champaign. Graduate School of Lib. & Information Science 1984 p43-57)

Nzotta. B. C. The social origins of librarians in developing countries: the case of Nigeria. charts *Int Libr Rev* 17:313-25 Jl '85

White. B. The librarian as intermediary [presented at LAIG study weekend] *Libr Assoc Rec* 87:340+ S '85

Librarianship as a profession

Burgett. M. L. Networking: a little-known area of librarianship can provide big benefits for those professionals willing to try it. *Technicalities* 5:3+ S '85

Foster. C. L. The shattered stereotype; the academic library in technological transition; presented at the 1983 ASIS Mid-year Meeting. ERIC Document Reproduction Service 1983 21p

Mosher, P. H. Quality and library collections: new directions in research and practice in collection evaluation (*In* Advances in librarianship, v13. Academic Press 1984 p211-38) bibl

Osburn, C. B. Toward a reconceptualization of collection development (*In* Advances in library administration and organization, v2, 1983. JAI Press 1983 p175-98)

Pankake. M. J. From book selection to collection management: continuity and advance in an unending work (*In* Advances in librarianship, v13. Academic Press 1984 p185-210) bibl

Rutstein. J. S. National and local resource sharing: issues in cooperative collection development [edited version of a paper delivered at the RTSD Collection Management and Development Institute, Irvine, Calif, September 1984] *Collect Manage* 7:1-16 Summ '85

Book selection

See Book selection

Cataloging

See Cataloging

Centralization

See Centralization of libraries

Circulation procedures

See Circulation procedures

Classification

See Classification

Directories

See also subhead Directories under the following subjects

Armed forces libraries

Information libraries, American

American library directory; edited by Jaques Cattell Press. 38th ed Bowker 1985 2v

Evaluation

Audunson, R. Brukerundersøkelser som redskap i evalueringsarbeid <User studies as an instrument in evaluation>. il *Bok Bibl* 50 no6:248-51 '83 sorg: en personlig synpunkt på biblioteksarbetet ‹Joys and sorrows of an information intermediary: a personal aspect of library work›. *Tidskr Dok* 40 nos2-3:93-4+ '84

Wilkinson. J. P. Subject divisionalism: a diagnostic analysis (*In* Advances in library administration and organization, v2. 1983. JAI Press 1983 p21-38)

Libraries

See also

Library service

  See also the following types of libraries

  College and university libraries

  County libraries

  National libraries

  Private libraries

  Public libraries

  Regional libraries

  Research libraries

  Rural libraries

  School libraries

  Special libraries

Acquisitions

See Acquisitions

Administration

See Administration

Aims and objectives

Libraries and the learning society: papers in response to A nation at risk: [by] Richard M. Dougherty and others. American Lib. Assn. 1984 146p

Book collections

See also

Overlap (library collections)

See also subhead Book collections under the following subjects

  College and university libraries

  Public libraries

  Research libraries

Collection development and management: the 1983 METRO Institute. *Collect Manage* 7:61-101 Spr '85

Hacken. R. D. Statistical assumption-making in library collection assessment: peccadilloes and pitfalls. *Collect Manage* 7:17-32 Summ '85

Lynden. F. C. Collection management (*In* The ALA yearbook of library and information services, v9, 1984. American Lib. Assn. 1984 p111-16)

effektivnosti ispol'zovaniia fonda ‹Circulation records as a measure of collection use›. charts *Sov Bibl* no2:52-63 '83

Owen. A. Output measures and state library development programs: a national survey. chart *Public Libr* 24:98-101 Fall '85

Robbins-Carter. J. B. and Zweizig. D. Are we there yet? Evaluating library collections, reference services, programs, and personnel. bibl *Am Libr* 16:624-7 O '85

Finance

See also

  Budgets

  Gale Research Company financial development award

  Government aid to libraries

See also subhead Finance under the following subjects

  College and university libraries

  National libraries

  Public libraries

Larssen. B. Opportune refleksjoner om nasjonal- og kulturøkonomi ‹Opportune reflections on national and cultural economics›. *Bok Bibl* 50 no6:236-7+ '83

Success stories; how 15 libraries raised money and public awareness; projects submitted for the 1983 Gale Research Company financial development award. American Lib. Assn. 1983 52p

History

See also subhead History under the following subjects

  College and university libraries

  Jewish libraries and collections

  Law libraries and collections

  Music libraries and collections

  Private libraries

  Public libraries

Calvert. P. J. The Levuka reading room: Fiji's first library. *J Libr Hist Philos Comp Libr* 20:302-9 Fall '85

Casteleyn. M. A history of literacy and libraries in Ireland; the long traced pedigree. Gower 1984 255p bibl il

Divnogortsev. A. L. Mezhdunarodnye sviazi sovetskikh bibliotek v 20-e gg; na primere deiatel'nosti VOKS ‹International ties with Soviet libraries in the 20's with special reference to the All-Union Society for Cultural Relations with Foreign Countries›. *Sov Bibl* no2:77-83 '83

FIGURE 6.5

Information networks—*cont.*

Denenberg, R. Linked systems project, part 2: standard network interconnection. charts *Libr Hi Tech* 3 no2:71-9 '85

McCallum, S. H. Linked systems project, part 1: authorities implementation. chart *Libr Hi Tech* 3 no2:61-8 '85

Sloan, B. G. The new age of linked systems. *Am Libr* 16:652+ O '85

Aims and objectives

Kunicki, M. L'organisation de réseaux d'information scientifique dans les pays aux possibilités restreintes: les prémisses <The organization of networks of scientific information in countries with restricted possibilities: premises>. bibl *Documentaliste* 21:18-22 Ja/F '84

Australia

Judge, P. J. Letter from Australia [current situation in information developments] chart *J Inf Sci* 9 no4:163-70 '84

Chile

Freudenthal, J. R. Toward a national information network in Chile (*In* Seminar on the Acquisition of Latin American Library Materials (27th: 1982: Washington, D.C.). Public policy issues and Latin American library resources. SALALM Secretariat 1984 p109-17)

Europe

Ekholm, K. and Luoma, A. Kulttuurin tietopalvelu Jyväskylään <Cultural information service in Jyväskylä>. *Kirjastolehti* 77 no4:184-5 '84

Great Britain

Shackel, B. Progress of the BLEND-LINC [Birmingham and Loughborough Electronic Network Development-Loughborough Information Network Community] electronic journal project (*In* International Association of Technological University Libraries. Meeting (10th: 1983: Essen, Germany). The future of serials. IATUL 1984 p69-82) charts

Latin America

Italy

Ercoli, P. Dati, informazioni, programmi: problemi di protezione <Data, information, programs: problems of protection>. il *Inf Doc* 11:6-16 Ja '84

Norway

Strøm, O. Dersom bibliotekpolitikk avfødte en informasjonspolitikk <If library policy results in an information policy>. *Bok Bibl* 50 no8:331-2 '83

Information science

See also
  Documentation
  Information theory

Guinchat, C. and Menou, M. J. General introduction to the techniques of information and documentation work. UNESCO Press 1983 340 p bibl il

Library and Information Technology Association (U.S.). National Conference (1st: 1983: Baltimore, Md.). Crossroads; proceedings of the first National Conference of the Library and Information Technology Association, September 17-21, 1983, Baltimore, Maryland; edited by Michael Gorman. American Lib. Assn. 1984 261p

Rajagopalan, T. S. and Rajan, T. N. Use of information in science and research with emphasis on national development: some Indian experiences. chart *Int Forum Inf Doc* 9:3-9 Jl '84

Ravichandra Rao, I. K. Quantitative methods for library and information science. Wiley Eastern 1983 271p il

Tague, J. Les sciences de l'information: aspects théoriques et interdisciplinaires <Information science: theoretical and interdisciplinary aspects>. chart *Argus* 13:5-9 Mr '84

Aims and objectives

Kochen, M. Impacts of microcomputers on information use patterns (*In* International Conference on the Application of Mini- and Micro-Computers in Information, Documentation and Libraries (1983: Tel Aviv, Israel). The application of mini- and micro-computers in

Information officers *See* Special librarians
Information policy

See also
Freedom of information
Information services—Legal aspects

Bearman, T. C. Information and productivity: implications for the library/information community (*In* The Bowker annual of library & book trade information. 30th ed Bowker 1985 p85-90)

Data protection: a practical conference for information managers; Aslib conference, London, 6-7 March 1985. *Aslib Proc* 37:293-337 Ag '85

Emmens, C. A. Cable Communications Policy Act. *SLJ* 32:120 O '85

Kelly, M. S. Information/reference [government information policy] *Tex Libr J* 61:86-7 Fall '85

Nelson, M. G. Flowing to the inverted pyramid [broad and equal opportunities for public access to information] *Wilson Libr Bull* 60:4 O '85

Wicklein, J. Will the new technologies kill the public library? (*In* Library and Information Technology Association (U.S.). National Conference (1st: 1983: Baltimore, Md.). Crossroads. American Lib. Assn. 1984 p34-40)

Zurkowski, P. The new information agenda in Washington: some case studies from the private sector viewpoint [with discussion] (*In* The Right to information. McFarland & Co. 1984 p37-53)

Australia
Judge, P. J. Letter from Australia [current situation in information developments] chart *J Inf Sci* 9 no4:163-70 '84

France
Pelou, P. L'informatisation des documents administratifs en France et l'information du citoyen <Computerization of government documents in France and the information of the citizen> [presented at the 1983 IFLA conference] *Bull Inf Assoc Bibl Fr* no122:15+ '84

Hungary
Földi, T. Decision-making and information provision in a centrally planned economy with a regulated market: the case of Hungary. *Int Forum Inf Doc* 9:31-2 Jl '84

Ireland
Cooper, R. The information matrix. charts *Libr Rev* 34:70-8 Summ '85

Legal aspects
See Information policy; Information services—Legal aspects

Philosophical aspects
Negrotti, M. How artificial intelligence people think: cultural premises of artificial intelligence community. charts *Inf Doc* 11:82-105 Ap '84

Research
See Research in information science

Social aspects
Diener, R. A. V. Conflicting societal visions on the nature of information: social, cultural, economic, and political perspectives (*In* 1984: challenges to an information society. Knowledge Industry Publs. 1984 p3-6) chart

Line, M. B. Quelques conséquences possibles de la technologie de l'information <A few possible outcomes of information technology>. *Bull Inf Assoc Bibl Fr* no122:7-9 '84

Rice, R. E. New patterns of social structure in an information society (*In* 1984: challenges to an information society. Knowledge Industry Publs. 1984 p30-3)

Shaw, D. J. and Dingle, S. M. Views of information from the Brave new world of 1984 (*In* 1984: challenges to an information society. Knowledge Industry Publs. 1984 p10-12) chart

Surprenant, T. T. Developing technologies and their impact on libraries: eight trends (*In* Library serials standards. Meckler 1984 p19-26)

Teaching
See also
Information scientists—Education
See also subhead Teaching under the following subjects
Automation of library processes
Information storage and retrieval

Armstrong, C. J. and Large, J. A. The design and implementation of a microcomputer teaching package for online bibliographic searching (*In* International Conference on the Application of Mini- and Micro-Computers in Information, Documentation and Libraries (1983: Tel Aviv, Israel). The application of mini- and micro-computers in information, documentation and libraries. North-Holland 1983 p189-94)

Er Norges bibliotekhøgskole født? <Is the Norwegian advanced library school born>. *Bok Bibl* 50 no6:268-9 '83

FIGURE 6.6

strated. A brief description of SIM-400M is included, with details of the system's modules which perform the following functions: creating, editing, updating, sorting, merging, searching, calculating, listing, index preparation, and generation of the database vocabulary. (E. M.)

UDC 025.4.036

85.12.329. **Design issues in a full text news and current affairs database** / Lynda Warrilow. — In: 7th Int. Online Inf. Meet. Oxford; New Jersey, s. a., 411-418.

Describes a full text retrieval service called World Reporter developed by Datasolve Ltd., UK. The World Reporter service which became operational in 1983, provides access to information from a variety of current affairs sources. The service's design criteria are discussed. Data capture issues are further discussed. The following information sources are accepted: 1) hard copy which can be entered into the database in a variety of ways, including keypunching and OCR scanning; 2) magnetic media, which are provided by some publishers of current affairs information who use computer-driven systems in the production of their publications; 3) computer-to-computer transmission, which

tures are identified, a typology of knowledge and basic components for knowledge classification are described. Key concepts in ES design are expounded and implementation examples are given. A brief review of the problem-oriented programming languages used in ESs is included. It is observed that some designers find it desirable to return to general-purpose programming languages, e. g. PASCAL. It is suggested that ESs be classified by the following aspects: application area, nature and implementation principles of problems, and control structure kind. Each aspect is discussed separately. Deeper treatment is accorded to control structures. Two other alternative approaches to classification are considered. The good effect that information science has had upon ES design is noted. The conclusion is that the use of ESs is likely to expand and that man-machine interaction will continue to develop. It is suggested that a considerable contribution to ES research and design is to be expected from the 15-year Japanese project that aims at working out the software and hardware components for a high-speed system called KNOWLEDGE/INFORMATION. The project relies on parallel processing techniques. (S. Sergeev) tion for retrieval of names, full texts or parts of documents is presented. The paper describes the system messages that are used as a communication tool between the computer system and the user, and concludes with a description of the terminal access facilities. (V. S.)

UDC 025.4.036:34

85.12.330. **Informatics and judicial decisions.** Informatica e decisione giudiziaria / Vittorio Novelli. — Inf. e diritto, 1984(1985), 10, No. 3, 131-137. — In Italian.
Discusses the use of computer-based information systems and databases in the judicial practice: in looking up legal norms, precedent information, in criminal investigations, etc. Latterly, computers and in particular expert systems have been used to evaluate witness and suspect evidence. The author touches upon the issue of confidentiality in criminal investigations drawing upon computer-processed data. The two areas in which informatisation of the judicial procedure appears to be most promising are the online bibliographic information systems (including full-text ones) on legal norms and factual systems on judicial decisions. Automating decision-making in law (notably in civil law) is unlikely in principle, because this is a purely human activity which should be cognizant of a multitude of nonformalisable or poorly formalisable factors — personality-related, psychological, or social. The author cautions about the possibility of worng estimates in the introduction of the computer in the judicial practice. (A. B.)

UDC [025.4.036:510.63]:65.012.122

85.12.331. **Expert systems** / K. K. Obermeyer. — In: Encycl. Libr. and Inf. Sci. Vol. 38. Suppl. 3. New York, N. Y.; Basel, 1985, 158-176. —40 refs.
The capabilities of expert systems (ES) in comparison with traditional information processing software tools are reviewed. Two criteria are suggested by which ESs are distinguished from conventional information systems and from the early DSSs. Main tasks in ES design are formulated. It is pointed out that the design of such systems has become a topical research area in AI. The global structure of the ES is presented. In discussing ES architecture, three types of struc-

Москва, 1983, 155-158. — In Russian.
The problem of optimal disk allocation of databases and optimisation of their presentation to users is reducible to a linear model and is solved by integer programming techniques. (A. G.)

UDC 681.3.068

85.12.333. **Using a description of parameter calculation algorithms for program design with due regard for computer resource limitations.** Использование описания алгоритмов расчета показателей для проектирования программ с учетом ограничений на ресурсы ЭВМ / А. Б. Лернер, С. М. Могилевский. — Классификаторы и док., 1985, № 5, 8-11. — In Russian. 5 refs.
Presents an approach to and methods for evaluating economic information processing algorithms, defining their optimisation domains during the early phases of program design, and discusses aspects of design based on the total use of these methods. The overall strategy and methods of optimisation domain definition are explored within the framework of the program design process. The resource estimation methods can be used to design programs on a variety of computers using different programming languages. They can be used to computerised the design of software of different purposes and levels. (V. E.)

UDC 002.53:681.327

85.12.334. **A general procedure for information system design using a DBMS.** Общая технология проектирования информационных систем с использованием СУБД / А. А. Симонов, А. М. Шиман. — В кн.: Автоматиз. исслед. на основе инф.-вычисл. сети. Ленинград, 1984, 158-169. — In Russian.
Presents a procedure for information system design which summarises the experience gained in the DBMS-based design and operation of several computerised information systems in production control. The overall design process is divided into six steps: (1) development of an infological model of the subject field; (2) determination of the database logical structure; (3) design of the database loading system; (4) implementation of the information system application functions on the database; (5) choice of optimal parameters of the database physical organisation; (6) design of a system for maintaining the information system's

Scientific and Technical Information in Moscow. An English version has been available since 1967, and the present title dates from 1971.

Informatics Abstracts appears monthly, and each year's issues comprise about 4,000 abstracts, each being of some 400 words generally, rather longer than those in *LISA*.

Over the last few years the origins of the items abstracted have changed significantly; in 1973 the service covered about 400 journals, and about three-quarters of the items included were originally in English, German or Russian. Since then the overall number of titles covered has expanded and increased, to over 1,300, as has the proportion of entries originating in other Eastern-bloc countries, and Japan. The coverage of Russian and Japanese journals will probably be the features that will appeal to the US or UK user, although the service covers most of the principal English-language and European journals. A recent survey (Stefaniak, 1985) covering the seven-year period 1977–1983 shows that 67 journals provide over 50 per cent of all papers cited; the top five of these journals are Russian (2), German (2) and Japanese. There is, however, a distinct emphasis on the scientific and technical library field and information handling, reflecting the bias towards those areas evident throughout the Soviet library and information profession. The time-lag between appearance of the original item and publication of the abstract varies enormously, but can be as little as four–six months. Postal delay to Western countries can, however, result in several months' delay between publication date and receipt.

The categories of material that *Informatics Abstracts* covers are wide; 66 per cent of the total abstracts are from journals of international origin, but the service also covers monographs, conference proceedings, reviews, patents, standards, and unpublished manuscripts deposited with VINITI.

The specimen page (Figure 6.6) shows the general appearance of *Informatics Abstracts*; abstracts are informative, and signed by the abstractor, or their origin otherwise indicated. Each entry begins with the abstract number – year and part followed by a running number, thus 85.12.329 is item 329 in the December 1985 issue. The main heading is the title, in English in our version, with an original language title (Cyrillic script is not transliterated). The author's name is given, but no description, the journal title, date (year only), volume, part and page number, and an indication of the original language. There is a note of the number of references cited, but no indication of illustrations or bibliography. Each entry, or group of entries, is prefixed by a UDC number, although this is not used for arrangement.

Each issue is arranged in a series of broad subject headings, as shown in the sample contents page (Figure 6.7). The scientific and technical emphasis will be immediately apparent. Each monthly part has an author index only, divided into two parts – Cyrillic and Roman alphabets. The final issue each year – number 12 – has a cumulated author index, and a subject index to the whole year's issues. This is a rotated index, generated by computer, and based on descriptors, but free indexing methods are used to determine the descriptors, there being no thesaurus in use. The specimen page of the 1985 subject index (Figure 6.8) shows the style of entry; reference is to the issue number in heavy type and the running number of the abstract, and includes a note of the country of origin where the content is specifically geographical.

Information Science Abstracts (ISA) began to appear in 1969, and is the successor to *Documentation Abstracts*, which started in 1966. Its present frequency is twelve issues per year. The principal sponsors of the publication are the American Society for Information Science, the American Chemical Society (Division of Chemical Information) and the Special Libraries Association, with other support from the American Society of Indexers, the American Library Association, the Association of Information and Dissemination Centers, the Association of Library and Information Science Education, and the Medical Library Association.

ISA is now published for Documentation Abstracts Inc. by Plenum Publishing Corporation; it is now appearing on schedule after a number of years when production was erratic and its editorial offices were in various locations. Monthly publication replaced the bimonthly schedule in 1984; the service is also available online via DIALOG (file 202). Delays between publication of original items and the appearance of the abstract are still longer than in other services, however. Bottle and Efthimiadis (1984) reckoned on an average delay of 27 months, and attributed this to *ISA*'s use of volunteer abstractors.

FIGURE 6.7

INFORMATICS ABSTRACTS

1985, vol. 23, No. 12

Abstracts 85.12.1—85.12.476

CONTENTS

Subsumed under Class 20 of the GASNTI Subject Authority

FIGURE 6.8

FIGURE 6.9

Abstracts Classification and Contents

INFORMATION SCIENCE
ABSTRACTS

formerly DOCUMENTATION ABSTRACTS

VOLUME 21, NO. 3 MARCH 1986
ABSTRACTS 86—2001 TO 86—3000

Published by Plenum Publishing Corporation, 233 Spring Street, New York. NY 10013 for., Documentation Abstracts, Inc. Founded by the American Society for Information Science (ASIS), the Division of Chemical Information of the American Chemical Society (DCI), and the Special Libraries Association (SLA). Currently guided also by the American Library Association (ALA), the American Society of Indexers (ASI), Association of Information and Dissemination Centers (ASIDIC), Association of Library and Information Science Education (ALISE) and the Medical Library Association (MLA). Other interested organizations are invited to participate.

Board of Directors, Documentation Abstracts, Inc.

Editorial correspondence should be addressed to H. Allcock, Editor, *Information Science Abstracts*, IFI/Plenum Data Corporation, 302 Swann Avenue, Alexandria, VA 22301.

Subscription orders and correspondence regarding subscriptions should be addressed to Circulation Department, Plenum Publishing Corporation, 233 Spring Street, New York, NY 10013.

Subscription rate for *Information Science Abstracts*, Volume 21, 1986 (12 issues), is $325 (outside U.S. $364). Individual (non-institutional) members of the American Society of Indexers, the American Society for Information Science, the Division of Chemical Information of the American Chemical Society, the Association of Library and Information Science Education, the Medical Library Association, and the Special Libraries Association are eligible for a reduced subscription rate of $95.00 per volume for personal use only.

Information Science Abstracts is published monthly, composed by Informonics, Inc. Littleton. MA. Copyright © 1986 by Documentation Abstracts, Inc. *Information Science Abstracts* is available online (DIALOG File 202).

Postmaster: Send address changes to *Information Science Abstracts*, Plenum Publishing Corporation. 233 Spring Street, New York, NY 10013.

Application to mail at Second Class Postage rates is pending at New York, NY, and at additional mailing offices.

FIGURE 6.10

Information Science—Documentation

1.0 General Aspects, Definitions

86-2001   Alexander, G.J.; Lunenfeld, H. (US Dept. of Transportation, Washington, DC [USA]). **A users' guide to positive guidance in highway control.** *In Information Design.,* 351-383 (1984). John Wiley & Sons Ltd., New York, NY. 8 ref. $89.95. ISBN: 0-471-10431-0.

This paper introduces the Positive Guidance approach needed to enhance the safety and efficiency of problem locations at relatively low cost. This approach, which is short-range and high-payoff, is based on the premise that drivers can be given sufficient information about hazards to enable them to perform their task error free. This approach joins the highway engineering and human factors technologies to produce an information system matched to the characteristics of the substandard location.

86-2002   Feather, J.P. (Dept. of Library and Information Studies, Loughborough Univ., England [UK]). **The book in history and the history of the book.** *Journal of Library History* 21(1), 12-26 (Win 1986).

The book as a revealing tool in the pursuit of history is the topic of this article. The physical characteristics of the book (presentation of a text); the definition of the size and constitution of the audience for books; the history of education and literacy are the basic topics used by the author to make his arguments for the book's impact on the passing on of facts, i.e. history. Data may be obtained through eighteenth century book

86-2007   Berry, J. **Tension, stress, and debate [Report on 1986 Conference of Association for Library and Information Science Education]** *Library Journal* 3(5), 29-31 (Mar 15, 1986).

Reports on 1986 Conference of the Association for Library and Information Science Education held in Chicago, Illinois, January 15-17. The theme was "Accreditation: The Way Ahead." Stress management for faculty, new paradigms, response from the practice, insights from educators and research, and program highlights are noted. (ERIC)

86-2008   Eastburn, W.N. **Hartford Convention, 1814-15 [Autographs]** *In Manuscripts: The First Twenty Years.,* 105-109 (1984). Greenwood Press, Westport, CT. ISBN: 0-313-24281-X.

The author recounts his experiences in trying to find autograph items from the Hartford Convention of 1814. A history of the Convention and the circumstances that led to it is provided. The author then outlines his strategy in mailing out for information on available documents, and reports on his success or failure in given areas.

86-2009   Harris, M.H. **History of libraries in the Western World.** 1984. Scarecrow Press, Inc. Metuchen, NJ. 289 p.

This book contains a bibliography of all current literature on the history of libraries in the West. A considerable body of new work in library history, especially American and English, is cited. Several specific aspects of the history of libraries in the West have been deleted in this second edition, in order to emphasize the general overview.

86-2010   Nash, J.D. **Bibliography of Hardware Description Lan-**

has something to learn and something to teach at every point at which the printed word impinges on the organization of society or on economic activity.

86-2003 Swezey, R.W. **Optimizing legibility for recall and retention.** In *Information Design.*, 145-156 (1984). John Wiley & Sons Ltd, New York, NY. 28 ref. $289.95. ISBN: 0-471-1043-0.

Though the author recognizes that such approaches as that of Biggs is a good starting point in meeting the need of applied research on methods of increasing and/or facilitating recall and retention of information, the author argues that research which differentially manipulates stimulus characteristics and assesses the effects on recall and retention is needed, and investigates this research in this paper.

86-2004 Wright, P. (MRC Applied Psychology Unit, Cambridge, England (UK)). **Informed design for forms.** In *Information Design.*, 545-577 (1984). John Wiley & Sons Ltd, New York, NY. 61 ref. ISBN: 0-471-1043-0.

This paper discusses practical remedies for poor form design, and considers three alternatives: the possibility of training designers in techniques for juggling the various constraints, the possibility of selecting good communicators in the first place, and the possibility of formulating a research programme that would provide the kind of inforamtion that could be put to practical use by forms designers. The paper also examines what potential design improvements arise from the research that has been done on forms.

86-2005 Zwaga, H.; Easterby, R. (Univ. of Utrecht, Utrecht [Netherlands]). **Developing effective symbols for public information.** In *Information Design.*, 277-297 (1984). John Wiley & Sons Ltd. New York, NY. 15 ref. $89.95. ISBN: 0-471-1043-0.,

This paper discusses some results of the decision to standardize the verbal description of the image for a symbol, and the feasibility of using this kind of image description. This chapter is specifically concerned with some of the evaluation techniques of proposed images for the symbols required, and the development of a reliable evaluation procedure.

See also 86-2675, 86-2678, 86-2826, 86-2929, 86-2967

1.1 Conferences, Publications, Bibliographies

86-2006 —**Confidence, competence, and control** [Summary of American Library Association 1986 Midwinter Meeting] *Library Journal* 3(5), 23-28 (Mar 15, 1986).

This article summarizes the 1986 Midwinter Meeting of the American Library Association (ALA) held in Chicago, Illinois, January 18-23. Discussion covers debate over Lacy Report, censorship, ALA's financial situation, divestiture and the ALA endowment, debate among ALA candidates, federal matters, continuing education, service to members, and strategic planning. (ERIC)

HDLs as tools, such as logic synthesis. In many cases, such papers offer some insight into HDLs, but they are generally not included in this bibliography.

86-2011 Wall, C.E., ed. *Library Hi-Tech bibliography*, **Volume 1.** 1986. Pierian Press, Ann Arbor, MI. 190 ISBN: 0-87650-219-2.

This volume contains annotated bibliograpies of publications which have appeared since July 1985 on the following topics: barcoding collections; use of computers in bibliographic instruction; cable television; computer courseware evaluations; managing library liability in disaster preparedness; electronic mail; library systems developed in house; interlibrary loan and document delivery; laser disc technology; local area networks; management information systems in libraries; microcomputer software; online public access catalogs; retrospective conversion; software review sources; telecommuting; turnkey systems; video display terminal hazards and ergonomic issues and word processing in libraries.

86-2012 White House Conference on Library and Information Services. **Five year review of progress made toward implementation of the resolutions adopted at the 1979 White House Conference of Library and Information Service.** Jan 1985. 73 p. ERIC. ED 258 573.

This report documents progress made toward the implementation of 55 of the 64 resolutions adopted by the delegates to the first White House Conference on Library and Information Services in 1979. It is noted that implementation of the resolutions has been occurring and continues to occur at various levels: some resolutions were implemented simply through communication to a specific governmental body, while others have been achieved through state of federal legislative or executive actions and through work by individuals, agencies, organizations, and associations. Due to the changing political and economic environment, some resolutions have had to be tabled until conditions change. The individual resolutions are presented in six categories: (1) Goals and Objectives—13 resolutions; (2) Organizatios and Finance—17 resolutions; (3) Technology, Resource Sharing and Education—18 resolutions; (4) Special Constituent Concerns—4 resolutions; (5) International Issues-6 resolutions; and (6) Conference Follow-up and Commendation —6 resolutions. The full text of each resolution is provided together with notes on implementation steps taken to date, agencies and organizations involved, and miscellaneous comments. (ERIC)

See also 86-2075, 86-2078, 86-2084, 86-2108, 86-2117, 86-2179, 86-2191, 86-2192, 86-2247, 86-2248, 86-2249, 86-2271, 86-2272, 86-2278, 86-2336, 86-2343, 86-2373, 86-2379, 86-2452, 86-2585, 86-2586, 86-2587, 86-2589, 86-2591, 86-2606, 86-2607, 86-2608, 86-2613, 86-2638, 86-2669, 86-2682, 86-2736, 86-2740, 86-2741, 86-2788, 86-2789, 86-2790, 86-2796, 86-2846, 86-2847, 86-2848, 86-2849, 86-2851, 86-2852, 86-2910, 86-2926, 86-2965, 86-2999

ISA overlaps only marginally with the other services described; LaBorie, Halperin and White (1985) found that 57 per cent of the journals abstracted are not covered by any other service. It is not limited exclusively to information science, although that is its principal area of concern. Its central feature is its coverage of report literature; about half of the abstracts published relate to ERIC, NTIS, patents, other non-serial sources, conference proceedings and monographs, which is a far higher proportion than in other services. About 10,000 abstracts are published each year, and although serials coverage is wide – about 450 titles – very few core titles are indexed cover-to-cover; in most cases only relevant articles are abstracted. The introductory page (Figure 6.9) gives an outline of coverage and arrangement.

The specimen page of abstracts (Figure 6.10) illustrates the main features of the arrangement; abstracts are grouped under broad subject headings. They are brief, usually 100–200 words, and their source is indicated if not in-house. The citation is under author, frequently with designation, with the title (in heavy type). Transliterations and translations are given for non-English-language material, and an indication of the original language. Journal information includes details of volume, part, page, date (including the month). There is an indication of illustrations, references or tables, and a note of the supporting body for research projects. Cross references are provided to other relevant abstracts in the same or previous issues of *ISA*, and this is a most valuable feature.

Each issue contains an author index and a subject index: these are merged into annual indexes which appear in the December issue. A cumulative index covering 1976–1979 has been separately published.

Bulletin Signalétique, Section 101 – Sciences de l'information/Documentation is a comprehensive abstracting service, compiled and published by Informascience, the Centre for Scientific and Technical Documentation in Paris, a part of the Centre National de la Recherche Scientifique. Section 101, which is available separately, is devoted to information science and documentation. It has been published since 1963, and its present title dates from 1972. Section 101 appears in 12 monthly parts, but in practice two pairs of issues are usually published together each year, giving a total of 10 issues, with a separate annual index. As well as a hard copy, a microfiche edition is available. *Bulletin Signalétique* is compiled and produced by an automated system –

PASCAL On-line (or PASCALINE) – and magnetic tapes are available, hence automated SDI services can be based on it, and retrospective searching can be carried out online.

The service is bilingual in part; the preliminary information, advice on usage, and classification scheme, which appear in each issue, are printed in two columns, the first French, the second English, and the indexes are similarly printed in two language versions. Even to the user confined to the English language the service therefore offers a great deal: items can be easily traced from an English language index, and although the abstracts themselves are in French, the majority of items cited are in fact of UK or US origin, and thus titles are given in English.

Section 101 covers monographs, journals, theses, standards and reports; about 100 journals are abstracted. Each year approximately 4,000–5,000 abstracts appear; these are usually brief, rarely more than 80 words, and frequently a single sentence. The main features of this service, for which the English-language user will need it, are firstly its excellent coverage of Western European literature, which is poorly represented in other services, and secondly its speed of abstracting and publication, often as low as a 10–12 week time-lag between publication of an original and the appearance of the abstract. As well as its strong European coverage, its speed makes it valuable also for UK and US literature, which is well represented, and generally comprises about two-thirds of the items abstracted.

Abstracts are arranged under subject headings, with an abstract number comprising year, number of section (always 101 in our case) and a running number. The citations give author's name and place of work, the title in the original language (except for non-Roman alphabets) and a translated title in French, although English titles remain untranslated. The journal titles are given and country of origin, date (year only), volume number, part, pages and an indication of bibliographies or references.

Each issue has its own indexes, which cumulate annually. A single author index is given, and separate subject indexes in French and English. The index is rotated, and terms cited often include the country of origin, so that it is possible in many cases to determine from the index the likely language of the original. As has been shown, use of this service poses very few problems to the English-language user, and its speed and coverage make it a valuable supplement to the other services discussed.

Although the major services we have discussed cover computerized aspects of library operations increasingly thoroughly, automation has become such an important and central issue in our fields that the sources of information on that aspect of library operations alone are worth considering; *Computer and Control Abstracts (CCA)* has often been regarded as suitable for a place with the other specialized services examined here. *CCA* is a publication of INSPEC – a service of the Institution of Electrical Engineers – and is not primarily concerned with librarianship and information science; however, of the 60,000 of more abstracts published each year as many as 3,000 may relate to mechanized information storage and retrieval. Headings include 'information science and documentation' which subsumes 'information storage and retrieval', and others of similar relevance. The main reason for consulting *CCA* would be its very rapid publication schedule: issues appear monthly and abstracts are often published within three months of the publication of an original item, and this is important in such a fast-moving subject area. Indexes in each issue of *CCA* lead the researcher to bibliographies, to conference proceedings and report literature; twice-yearly subject indexes are published separately. The spread of titles covered by *CCA* is unexpected in view of its title, and thus the quantity of relevant material is high.

To conclude this chapter, although strictly outside our scope, we might remember that several other services are produced around the world to control library and information science literature; Marco (1983, pp. 51–3) notes the existence of a number of national sources. One important title is the West German *Nachrichten für Dokumentation*: this is produced six times a year, and comprises feature articles, each of which has an abstract in English as well as German, then contents lists of information science journals – useful because it includes a number of European and Japanese journals not so readily available for scanning elsewhere, and finally brief abstracts of current contents of German and Austrian information science journals (Schrifttum zur Informationswissenschaft und praxis) divided by broad subjects.

Two other services which might be of general interest and which are both published in English are *Hungarian Library and Information*

Science Abstracts, published in Budapest, which is a useful Eastern European source, and *Indian Library Science Abstracts*, published in Calcutta and recording articles from Indian library periodicals and Indian conference proceedings; this latter title is more fully described elsewhere (Prytherch and Satija, 1986).

7   Wider sources

The previous chapter concentrated on those abstracting and indexing services that specialize in librarianship and information science. These fields, however, cannot be regarded in isolation: libraries and information units are a part of far larger complexes – an industrial firm, a school, college or university, or, in the case of a public library, a community environment, having social, recreational and educational roles. To seek information about these fields from specialized sources alone is a blinkered approach; the context of the service provided offers valuable insights into the purpose and use of that service, and at times of economic difficulty it is vital to be able to argue the value of libraries and information units with evidence from the widest possible sources.

Clearly, some areas of activity will be more productive of information than others; for example, libraries and books have an important role in education at all levels, and this is reflected in educational journals, where articles on books, reading and libraries are not uncommon. This field is also well indexed and thus information can be readily traced. By contrast, the context of public library services is harder to define and more difficult to trace: articles on community services, social problems, welfare, leisure and amenity services often have little or nothing to say about libraries, yet the profession might feel that they should. Such areas are also scattered by various fields of publishing, and by the very general nature of their appeal: these factors make it awkward to identify which indexing services might be productive. Articles on community advice centres might appear in political journals, in social work journals, or in general newspaper articles: none of these journals would be covered by our specialized services, but neither would they necessarily be covered by any one other source.

FIGURE 7.1

LIBRARIES. Colleges of education. Owerri. Nigeria
Alvan Ikoku College of Education. *Library, 1963-1983*
A catalogue of the Historical Association collection of outdated
development / W.O. Emezi. — *Educ. Libr. Bull.*, Vol.27, no.2 :
Summer 84. — p9-21
Bibliography: p21

LIBRARIES. Educational institutions
— *North America*
Education libraries in the United States / Susan Baughman. —
Educ. Libr. Bull., Vol.27, no.2 : Summer 84. — p1-8
Bibliography: p8

LIBRARIES. Further education institutions
Implications of curriculum innovation
New curricula : educational implications and impact on
learning-centred resources / Eric Fletcher. — *Coombe Lodge Rep.*
, Vol.17, no.3 : 84. — p79-86
Student-Centred Learning Resources. — Bibliography: p86

LIBRARIES. Further education institutions
Libraries & resource centres. Assessment. Methodology
Evaluative frameworks for ensuring quality in the provision and
management of learning resources / Derek Marsh. — *Coombe
Lodge Rep.*, Vol.17, no.3 : 84. — p112-127
Student-Centred Learning Resources

LIBRARIES. Further education institutions
Provision — Standards
The Library Association's guidelines for college libraries : an
approach to resourcing and assessment / Rennie McElroy. —
Coombe Lodge Rep., Vol.17, no.3 : 84. — p87-94
Student-Centred Learning Resources. — Bibliography: p94

LIBRARIES. Further education institutions
Role
Professional co-operation : an area for development / W.A.
Tovell. — *Educ. Libr. Bull.*, Vol.28, pt 2 : Summer 85. — p2-4

LIBRARIES. Grammar schools
1600-1700
School libraries and librarianship in the early seventeenth century
/ D.K. Shearing. — *Asp. Educ.*, No.31 : 84. — p66-91
Aspects of Education: 1600-1750. — Bibliography: p87-9]

LIBRARIES. Higher education institutions
Development. Role of Council for National Academic Awards
Library development : the polytechnics / Wilfred Ashworth. —
Libr. Rev., Vol.33 : Autumn 84. — p132-138
The Council for National Academic Awards : The Library Dimension

Historical Association. *Library. Stock: History. Textbooks,
1870-1914 — Catalogues*
A catalogue of the Historical Association collection of outdated
history text-books first published before 1915. — *Hist. Educ. Soc.
Bull.*, No.33 (Supplement) : Spring 84. — 34p
The Historical Association collection of outdated history text-books is on
permanent personal loan to Professor G.R. Batho and is housed in the
School of Education of the University of Durham. The collection, which
contains over 3,000 volumes, covers works published from 1868 onwards
and has been supplemented by gifts from a number of sources, including
Mylon School, Warwick (per Mr. P.M. Bolton), Spennymoor
Comprehensive School (per Mr. E. Stephenson), Durham County Libraries
(per Mr. P. Burns), and Miss G.A. Williams (formerly Principal of
Doncaster College of Education). Appended is a catalogue of the holdings
from before the First World War. Enquiries for consultation, which can
only be made to Professor G.R. Batho, School of
Education, University of Durham, Leazes Road, Durham DH1 1TA

History text-books, 1870-1914 : a note on the Historical
Association collection at Durham / Gordon R. Batho. — *Hist.
Educ. Soc. Bull.*, No.33 : Spring 84. — p7-16
Bibliography: p16

LIBRARIES. Primary schools
Provision
The establishment of a school library / Kathleen Hactor. — *Sch.
Libr.*, Vol.32, no.4 : Dec 84. — p317-320

LIBRARIES. Schools
The appalling state of school libraries — a tragedy in many acts /
Colin Pidgeon. — *Sch. Libr.*, Vol.33, no.2 : Jun 85. — p101-103

School libraries : the foundations of the curriculum / by Eric
Williams. — *Insp. Advice*, Vol.21, no.1 : Summer 85. — p4-6
Bibliography: p6

School libraries : the way ahead / by Jenny Parmenter. — *Insp.
Advice*, Vol.21, no.1 : Summer 85. — p6-9
Bibliography: p9

LIBRARIES. Schools
Applications of microcomputer systems
An Apple in the library / Brian Earl. — *Sch. Libr.*, Vol.33, no.1 :
Mar 85. — p12-17

LIBRARIES. Schools
Effects of microelectronic devices
What price information? / Gwen Gawith. — *Educ. Libr. Bull.*,
Vol.27, no.2 : Summer 84. — p38-42
Reply to 'Will 1984 change anything?' Educ. Lib. Bull. Vol.27, no 1 :
Spring 1984   Bibliography: p42

Similarly articles on the role of libraries in specialized areas, such as the health service, may be concealed if we take a specialized approach. Medical information and libraries can be discussed in the medical press; a topic such as *bibliotherapy* may appear in the library press, the medical press, nursing journals or social work journals.

The essential advice to the researcher whose field is not to be confined to bare technique or simple description is to consider the context in which the service operates and identify sources which cover activity in those areas. Some of the sources likely to be most productive will now be considered.

British Education Index (BEI) is compiled within the Brotherton Library, University of Leeds, and indexes about 260 English journals available in Britain. A glance at the list of journals covered, which is given in each issue, reveals that very few would fall within the net of any of the specialized services we examined. Therefore many items found in *BEI* are likely to be new information if we have searched only in the specialized services.

The cumulated annual volume each year usually has forty or so direct references to *libraries* – the entries in the 1985 volume are shown here (Figure 7.1) to demonstrate the coverage and layout.

Further relevant material may be traced under headings such as *information* and *resources*. *BEI* is extremely easy to use; the typography is excellent, and the PRECIS method of indexing using controlled terms allows successful searches to be carried out quickly. From late 1987 *BEI* will be available online.

Educational Resources Information Center (ERIC): ERIC was founded in 1966, and is an official United States network of clearinghouses established to control all aspects of education. Two basic serial publications are issued: the *Current Index to Journals in Education (CIJE)* indexes and abstracts about 25 librarianship and information science journals, as well as all other important US journals in the field of education; it is the second serial, however, that is of greater value for our purposes: *Resources in Education (RIE)*. *RIE* indexes, abstracts and makes available research reports, descriptions of research programmes, conference papers and other kinds of published, semi-published and unpublished material.

Each of the 16 clearinghouses may submit material relevant to our fields, but the Information Resources Clearinghouse (ERIC/IR) will be the most central. ERIC/IR, which is located at Syracuse University, New York, covers all aspects of librarianship and information science, and includes educational technology and some aspects of systems analysis. The sample page (Figure 7.2) shows that each abstract consists of 100–150 words, and is preceded by a list of assigned descriptors. A substantial thesaurus of *ERIC Descriptors* is available from Oryx Press (11th ed., 1986). The sample entry (Figure 7.3) explains the full range of information that each résumé provides.

Because of the large number of entries within each clearinghouse section, and because other clearinghouses may submit material relevant to searches in our field, a subject index is provided in each issue of *RIE*, and a specimen page is reproduced here (Figure 7.4). A semi-annual index is available from 1982, and an annual index is published by Oryx Press. *RIE* has been available online for several years, via DIALOG and SDC.

For almost all of the items indexed, *ERIC* makes a microfiche copy available; for some items hard copy may also be obtained via *ERIC*, or, in the case of fully published material, from the publisher. Full collections of microfiche are maintained by hundreds of US institutions, and by key libraries elsewhere. A list of all the collections is printed at the end of each issue of *RIE* – in the UK the British Library Document Supply Centre maintains a collection and can produce a copy on demand for virtually all *ERIC* items.

The tremendous importance of *ERIC* cannot be overemphasized; as well as providing abstracts of fugitive material covered by no other service, it also provides the means of physically obtaining the items with the minimum of delay.

Research into Higher Education Abstracts covers about 250 journals, of international scope, including many North American titles. It is compiled in the UK by the Society for Research into Higher Education, published by Carfax Publishing Company, and is of obvious relevance to librarians in the higher and further education area who need information on the planning and policies of their institutions. A section in each issue is devoted to 'information networks' and this includes material on libraries.

FIGURE 7.2

104   Document Resumes

a 1978 study shows an increase in southeastern academic librarians' educational credentials. The report concentrates on the acceptability and significance of earning additional degrees, including the influence level of additional graduate level, hiring decisions, hiring at the administrative level, determining salary at the time of hiring, and determining periodic salary increases. (THC)

ED 267 816   IR 051 477
Woods, Elaine
GaIN: The Georgia Interactive Network for Medical Information.
Pub Date—25 Oct 85
Note— 11p. Paper presented at the Annual Meeting of the Georgia Library Association (Augusta, GA, October 25, 1985).
Pub Type— Reports - Descriptive (141) — Speeches/Meeting Papers (150)
EDRS Price - MF01/PC01 Plus Postage.
Descriptors—Academic Libraries, Database Management Systems, *Databases, Information Retrieval, *Information Science, Library Automation, *Library Networks, *Medical Libraries, *Medical Services, *Online Systems, Program Descriptions, Technological Advancement
Identifiers— *Georgia
    Five years ago, the National Library of Medicine (NLM) funded the Association of American Medical Colleges (AAMC) study of the impact of new

ing of the Georgia Library Association (Augusta, GA, October 25, 1985).
Pub Type— Opinion Papers (120) — Speeches/Meeting Papers (150)
EDRS Price - MF01/PC01 Plus Postage.
Descriptor—Computer Literacy, Futures (of Society), Information Needs, *Information Science, *Information Scientists, *Information Services, Information Utilization, Library Education, *Library Planning, Library Role, *Library Science, *Linking Agents, Position Papers, Technological Advancement
    The approaching information age will encompass a different societal system in the 21st century due to the impact of the information revolution resulting from developments in computer and communication technology. In light of these changes, libraries need to evolve with the new technology by preparing now to become part of the electronic revolution. Librarians must become familiar with all aspects of the communication cycle and its relationship with the organizations and communities to be served; they need to educate themselves about future scenarios relating to employment, education, energy, leisure, communications, etc., and the impact of changes on the role of the library; and they need to know the changing human needs of the information society, and how these needs will effect changes in characteristics of the library system. In the future, emphasis on a customized approach to designing

*Staff Development
Identifiers— *South Africa
    A study was undertaken to ascertain the position of inservice training for librarians in South Africa and to determine what adjustments were necessary for inservice training practice in South African libraries. An examination of the literature on inservice training revealed current trends, and the literature in the field of library science was analyzed against this background. A questionnaire was then compiled and sent to 63 South African libraries to determine to what extent these libraries approached the ideal situation as portrayed in the literature. Replies were received from 50 libraries and were analyzed according to library type. A brief review of the full study, this document is divided into the following sections: (1) a general introduction, including a definition of inservice training; (2) aims of training including the provision of necessary knowledge, guidance of staff toward greater insight, improvement of skills and broadening of experience, and development of a positive attitude towards work; (3) who should be responsible for inservice training; (4) possible cooperative training efforts; (5) differentiation of training; (5) a brief review of training methods, including applications in South African libraries; and (6) a scenario of the ideal situation. (THC)

ED 267 821   IR 051 482

facilitate the flow and use of the world's knowledge base in carrying out the functions of education, patient care, and management. GaIN (Georgia Interactive Network for Medical Information) responds to that challenge and speaks directly to many of the final recommendations issued in the report: GaIN is built upon an automated academic health sciences library; it is a gateway to external databases; and it uses database management concepts to organize, package, and deliver information to a multi-level network of users. This document describes the organization and funding of GaIN; key principles incorporated into the network; roles of GaIN members; management and administration of the network; GaIN services; and an evaluation of the program to be conducted in 1986. (THC)

ED 267 817   IR 051 478
Margai, Sarla R.
Future Challenges in Library Science.
Pub Date—25 Oct 85
Note—12p.; Paper presented at the Annual Meeting of the Georgia Library Association (Augusta, GA, October 25, 1985).
Pub Type— Opinion Papers (120) — Speeches/Meeting Papers (150)
EDRS Price - MF01/PC01 Plus Postage.
Descriptors—Computer Literacy, Decision Making, Information Networks, *Information Science, Information Scientists, *Information Services, Library Agents, Online Systems, Position Papers, Technological Advancement
This paper considers a number of potential developments for the future of library science and the roles of information professionals. Among the projections are: (1) the use of computers and management science operations research methodologies will form the basis of decision making in libraries in the future; (2) a concerted effort will be made to emphasize quality more than quantity to replace the present 'economy oriented formulae' with performance-based formulae; (3) information services will be more expensive; (4) specialists will tend to bypass middlemen; (5) there will be greater cooperation between the producers and the consumers of information; and (6) computers will enable library administrators to develop a better understanding and appreciation of information services among legislators, higher education commissioners, and private benefactors to procure adequate funding. (Author/THC)

ED 267 818   IR 051 479
Smalik, Mary L.
The Library Profession in the 21st Century: Transformation for Survival.
Pub Date—85
Note—16p.; Paper presented at the Annual Meet-

group practitioners. Libraries should act as centers where users can receive instruction in the uses of new communications technology; assistance in exploiting various databases; and important communication information services. (THC)

ED 267 819   IR 051 480
Agnew, Grace And Others
The Online Catalog and Patron Search Strategies at Georgia State University.
Pub Date—25 Oct 85
Note—20p.; Paper presented at the Annual Meeting of the Georgia Library Association (Augusta, GA, October 25, 1985).
Pub Type— Reports - Research (143) — Speeches/Meeting Papers (150)
EDRS Price - MF01/PC01 Plus Postage.
Descriptors—Academic Libraries, Higher Education, *Information Needs, *Library Catalogs, Library Research, *Online Searching, *Online Systems, *Search Strategies
Identifiers—Georgia State University, *Library Users, *Online Catalogs
An online catalog was introduced at Georgia State University in September 1985. Prior to its introduction, a study was conducted at Pullen Library to prepare for bibliographic instruction for catalog use. In the summer of 1985, 50 patrons were observed and interviewed as they used the library's card and/or computer output microfiche (COM) catalog. Patrons were observed to determine the kind and amount of information needed, the search strategies employed, and the results obtained. The researchers then applied these search strategies to the online catalog to discover the benefits and disadvantages of an online system, and to modify search strategies to maximize use of the online catalog. The most useful features of the online catalog, as discovered in this study, include: searching by keyword/term; using Boolean operators to link terms; limiting search results by date of publication, type of material, or language; and searching by class number. (Author/THC)

ED 267 820   IR 051 481
Vink, C. M.
In-Service Training in South African Libraries. A Brief Review Based on a Thesis for the M.Bibl. Degree of the University of Pretoria.
Pub Date—79
Note—10p.
Pub Type— Opinion Papers (120) — Reports - Re-
EDRS Price - MF01/PC01 Plus Postage.
Descriptors—Developing Nations, *Inservice Education, *Libraries, Library Cooperation, *Library Personnel, Library Research, *On the Job Training, Position Papers, Professional Development,

Pub Type— Reference Materials - Directories/Catalogs (132) — Reports - Descriptive (141)
EDRS Price - MF01/PC02 Plus Postage.
Descriptors—Career Planning, *Disabilities, Employment Services, *Federal Programs, *Higher Education, Information Networks, Information Services, Job Search Methods, Job Training, *Referral, State Programs, *Student Financial Aid
Disabled students preparing for the transition from high school to working life will find current, practical information in this reference circular, which was prepared to facilitate the transition to higher education or directly to a work situation. The information is arranged according to three basic transition models: (1) without special services; (2) with time-limited services; and (3) with ongoing services. The first section includes: Sources of Financial Aid for Disabled College Students; College Handbooks of Interest to Disabled Students; Handicapped Students' Rights under Federal Law; and Books in Special Media on Career Planning and Job Searching. The second section includes discussions and references on: Job Training, Placement, and Career Matching Services; Employment Networks Program; State Vocational Rehabilitation Agencies; and the Randolph-Sheppard Vending Facility Program. The third section includes discussions and references to nationally and locally supported employment programs. Information relating to all three models in the fourth section includes brief descriptions of adapted and special equipment and sources for additional information, as well as a reprint of The Rehabilitation Act of 1973, as Amended, Sections 501, 502, 503, and 504, Subpart B. (THC)

ED 267 822   IR 051 483
Redmond, Linda, Comp.
Sources of Braille Reading Materials. Reference Circular No. 86-2.
Library of Congress, Washington, D.C. National Library Service for the Blind and Physically Handicapped.
Pub Date—Nov 85
Note—19p.
Pub Type— Reference Materials - Directories/Catalogs (132)
EDRS Price - MF01/PC01 Plus Postage.
Descriptors—*Books, Braille, Publishing Industry, *Reading Materials, *Tactile Adaptation, Textbooks, Visual Impairments
This reference circular lists sources of braille books available for loan, purchase, rental, or free (give-away) distribution. Divided into four sections, it includes general sources of braille books, sources of specialized braille materials, the major braille presses, and resources for further information about

FIGURE 7.3

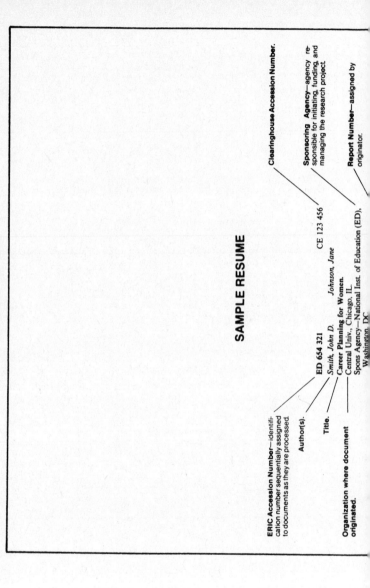

SAMPLE RESUME

ERIC Accession Number—identification number sequentially assigned to documents as they are processed.

Clearinghouse Accession Number.

Author(s).

ED 654 321   CE 123 456

Smith, John D.   Johnson, Jane

Title.

Organization where document originated.

Career Planning for Women.
Central Univ., Chicago, IL.
Spons Agency.—National Inst. of Education (ED), Washington, DC

Sponsoring Agency—agency responsible for initiating, funding, and managing the research project.

Report Number—assigned by originator.

Ave., Chicago, IL 60690 ($3.25).

Language—English, French

Pub Type—Speeches/Meeting Papers (150)

EDRS Price—MF01/PC06 Plus Postage.

Descriptors — Career Guidance, *Career Planning, Careers, *Demand Occupations, *Employed Women, *Employment Opportunities, Females, Labor Force, Labor Market, *Labor Needs, Occupational Aspiration, Occupations

Identifiers — Consortium of States, *National Occupational Competency Testing Institute

Women's opportunities for employment will be directly related to their level of skill and experience and also to the labor market demands through the remainder of the decade. The number of workers needed for all major occupational categories is expected to increase by about one-fifth between 1980 and 1990, but the growth rate will vary by occupational group. Professional and technical workers are expected to have the highest predicted rate (39 percent), followed by service workers (35 percent), clerical workers (26 percent), sales workers (24 percent), craft workers and supervisors (20 percent), managers and administrators (15 percent), and operatives (11 percent). This publication contains a brief discussion and employment information concerning occupations for professional and technical workers, managers and administrators, skilled trades, sales workers, clerical workers, and service workers. In order for women to take advantage of increased labor market demands, employer attitudes toward working women need to change and women must: (1) receive better career planning and counseling, (2) change their career aspirations, and (3) fully utilize the sources of legal protection and assistance that are available to them. (SB)

FIGURE 7.4

Subject Index

Conceptual Palette.   ED 268 019

Legal Responsibility
Research Interactions between Industry and
Higher-Education: An Examination of the Major
Legal Is es Involved in Four Repre-entative
Contract   ED 267 689

Legislation
An Over ew on Missing Children. Hearing before the Subcommittee on Children, Family,
Drugs a. Alcoholism of the Committ. on Labor and Human Resources. United States Senate,
Ninety-th Congress, First Session Review
of Progr . Made on the Plight of Missing Children, and the Involvement of Businesses, Corpo-
rations, and Organizations in the Search for
Missing Children.   ED 267 305

Legislators
A Survey of U.S. Senators Regarding Their High
School Education.   ED 267 956

Lesbianism
Lesbianism: Affirming Non-Traditional Roles.
                                        ED 267 367

Lesson Observation Criteria

Library Collections
Collection Mapping in School Library Media
Centers.

High School Students Gui e to Sources.
                                        ED 267 775

Passages to Fami. Histor   A Guide to Genea-
logical Research in the   mouth College Library.

Secondary Scien: Educe Library Resources
at New England' Teacher ducation Programs.
                                        ED 268 008

Library Cooperati n
The NABRIN R port of the National
Advisory Board on Rural Information Needs
Planning Committee.   ED 267 804

Library Education
Education and Change: Academic Librarians for
the 21st Century.   ED 267 815

Information and Productivity–Implications for
Education and Training. Report of a Joint UK/US
Seminar (1st Cranfield, England, July 27-30,
1984).

A Model Curriculum for the Education and
                                        ED 267 903

Limited English Speaking   211

Library 2000.   ED 267 818

Preservation at Stony Brook. Preservation Planning Program. Study Report.   ED 267 814

A Preservation Program for the Colorado State
University Libraries. The Final Report of the
ARL/OMS Preservation Planning Program.
                                        ED 267 809

Principles for the Preservation and Conservation
of Library Materials. IFLA Professional Reports,
No. 8.   ED 267 808

Library Research
Use of Personal Space in Libraries: A Review.
                                        ED 267 823

Library Science
The Library Profession in the 21st Century:
Transformation for Survival.   ED 267 806

Library Services
Development of a Strategic Plan for the Harold B.
Lee Library: A Model for the Library Public Ser-
vices.   ED 267 818

Exhibits in ARL Libraries. SPEC Kit 120.
                                        ED 267 813

Educational Technology Abstracts (ETA) is also published by Carfax Publishing Company and started in 1985; it covers about 230 journals in the fields of educational technology, the media, appropriate training, and educational aspects of computing. It is therefore an important source for topics such as resource centres, student-centred learning, distance learning – all of which have important implications for librarians.

Child Development Abstracts and Bibliography is published for the Society for Research in Child Development by the University of Chicago Press and will interest school and children's librarians; it includes a considerable amount of information on reading and early educational development.

Children's Literature Abstracts is published by the Children's Libraries Section of the International Federation of Library Associations. It covers journals from several countries, and produces abstracts of not more than 100 words, compiled by local correspondents in each country. The abstracts are in English, and although librarianship as such is excluded, they include much relevant material, for example on children's book publishing, children's authors, the psychological, educational and social criteria for children's books, which school and children's librarians will recognize as highly important. Many of the English-language journals abstracted are covered by the specialized services, but the simpler arrangement of *Children's Literature Abstracts*, the concise subject area, and the international perspective make it a significant source for those working in this field.

British Humanities Index (BHI) is published by the Library Association, and indexes about 300 English language journals in the field of 'the humanities', which is inevitably a field with no clear boundaries. The list of journals includes leading British newspapers – *The Times, Guardian, Observer* and *Sunday Times* – and the 'heavy' weeklies – *Spectator, Listener, New Society, New Statesman,* as well as far more obscure and specialized titles.

There are usually several entries under *libraries* in each issue, and usually from sources most unlikely to have been cited by one of the specialized services – for example, from newspapers, literary journals, local government sources, the architectural, archaeological, musical, and historical press.

Public Affairs Information Service Bulletin is compiled within the New York Public Library by Public Affairs Information Service Inc. Its topics include social conditions, and public administration; each issue usually has some 20–30 items directly relevant to our fields, and often from unexpected sources. The service includes government publications, and reports of public and private agencies as well as books, pamphlets and journal articles.

Social Science Citation Index is compiled by the Institute for Scientific Information Inc., of Philadelphia. When an article in a certain field of interest has proved valuable, use of *SSCI* can trace further work on the same topic by locating articles which cite the original piece in their list of references. This is a fast route to more information, particularly if the original article is concerned precisely with the required field. Librarianship is within its coverage, and the subject index of any issue will show extensive treatment.

Social Sciences Index is a publication of the H. W. Wilson Company; it covers some 350 general and sociological journals, predominantly of US origin, and includes items on the role of libraries in an educational and social context.

Sociological Abstracts, a publication of Sociological Abstracts Inc. of San Diego, has an international coverage on many aspects of sociology and management of interest to librarians. These include community development, social organization, mass culture, urban and rural deprivation, and leisure. The operation of groups and teams is also the subject of one of its sections.

The Library Association launched a new abstracting service ASSIA (*Applied Social Sciences Index and Abstracts*) in 1987. This is to cover some 500 journals internationally but with a British emphasis and will include such topics as the inner cities, social, moral, legal questions, handicapped and deprived groups – the elderly, disabled, prison populations and others – and should prove relevant and valuable in several library and information contexts.

Personnel and Training Abstracts is compiled in the UK by ANBAR Management Publications in association with the Institute of Personnel Management. Its coverage of training methods and evaluation, staffing policies and personnel selection, and management will make it valuable to anyone concerned with staff supervision or development.

Current Technology Index (CTI), which before 1981 was titled *British Technology Index*, is compiled and published by the Library Association. It indexes about 350 English-language journals in the fields of engineering, general technology, chemical technology, applied science, manufacturing and technical services. The list of journals published at the beginning of each issue reveals that no title covered would normally be scanned by any of the specialized services. *CTI* is relevant to our field in a number of ways; technical aspects of building are included, and thus the lighting, heating and ventilation of libraries can be researched here; technical processes in printing and papermaking are also included; data transmission, PRESTEL, computing and information retrieval also feature regularly. *CTI* is available online via DIALOG (File 142).

For automation and computing, sources were mentioned at the end of the previous chapter: these should now be included with other major sources, as the subjects have become a part of the core area of librarianship and information science rather than part of the wider fringe.

This chapter has mentioned only a small number of sources likely to prove productive of information. To trace further sources both within librarianship and information science, and in the wider fields of which our profession is an integral part, it is advisable to consult the basic bibliographical guides to find the principal abstracting and indexing tools in the relevant subject area.

Magazines for libraries (compiled by Bill Katz, 5th ed., Bowker 1986) is a very valuable source for this kind of search. The opening main section of the volume – 'abstracts and indexes' – lists some 200 and more services; each entry has a full citation and an annotation of 150 words indicating coverage, editorial policy and main features. The annotations are critical, and inclusion in the volume is in any case selective, so that only valuable titles are given. The rest of the volume is arranged under broad subject headings, with an index of titles at the end. Each main section commences with a subsection entitled 'basic abstracts and indexes', thus for any sought area the essential sources of further information can be readily identified.

Some sections deal with topics very close to our core areas – such as *Bibliography, Books and book reviews, Computers and automation*, and *Library periodicals*. Any of the other sections could have relevance to librarians and information workers in particular contexts: there are large sections on *Children,* which includes children's literature, *Communication, speech and media,* which includes aspects of audio-visual librarianship, *Cultural–Social studies* and *Education,* which will concern public librarians and librarians in the educational fields respectively. Serial librarians will be interested in the section on *Alternatives,* which includes alternative newspapers and the alternative press, *Little magazines* and *Serials.* These cited headings form only a very small proportion of the whole volume, and personnel in special services will find valuable source material on the subject areas with which they are concerned.

Ulrich's International Periodicals Directory (25th ed., Bowker 1986) is also a useful source, although no annotations are provided for any entry. Ulrich has sections on *bibliographies* and on *Library and Information Sciences,* but for the purposes of this chapter the significant feature is that for each subject area at the conclusion of the main sequence of entries and before any subheadings are treated is a subsection devoted to *abstracting, bibliographies, statistics.* This subsection will provide a ready guide to the indexing services available for consultation in that area; the coverage is international, and no critical apparatus is given, so care must be taken not to devote a disproportionate amount of energy to locating physically what may prove to be a service of small value. Online access is available to this service via DIALOG, ESA-IRS and BRS. A CD-ROM version is also to be issued.

A. J. Walford's *Guide to Reference Materials* (3 vols: Library Association, Vol. 1, 4th ed., 1980; Vol. 2, 4th ed., 1982; Vol. 3, 4th ed., 1986) also leads easily into information services in each subject area; every main section begins with a sub-division on *bibliographies* which includes principal bibliographies and indexing services for that subject. Each entry is given a brief annotation.

Similarly, Eugene P. Sheehy's *Guide to Reference Books* (American Library Association 10th ed., 1987) begins each subject area with a preliminary note of the key abstracting and indexing services, then describes general works, under the subheadings *guides, bibliography, current periodicals, indexes, dictionaries* and *encyclopedias,* enabling the researcher to locate the essential bibliographical services readily. Each item cited is given a brief annotation.

Through use of these and other similar sources, as well as the services itemized previously, it should be possible to trace information on the operational context of any type of library or information unit, to supplement material gathered from the chief specialized services.

8   Theses, dissertations and reports

Much of the theoretical examination of librarianship and information science has taken the form of research carried out in academic institutions. Traditionally, higher degrees required a thesis or dissertation, but now even at undergraduate level or on postgraduate 'taught' courses students are expected to produce lengthy projects or reports of a size and standard comparable to dissertations at master's level. What that standard is may not be clear; academic research is only as good as the supervision provided, and there have often been doubts on the relevance of topics, the mediocrity of some work, and the enormous quantity of material produced. In recent years the expansion of higher education and the enhanced level of librarianship and information science qualifications have led to the production of several thousand pieces of academic research each year in these fields alone. Whatever the overall standard, the argument runs that some of it is definitely of very high quality, and much more probably is.

But the definition of research in our practical profession has been widened: libraries, publishers, professional associations and other bodies now carry out research for their own purposes unallied to an academic qualification. This category of research may have a greater claim to practical value than its academic counterpart, and yet is often overlooked by guides to conventional thesis-type literature. This chapter is therefore concerned with all kinds of research – academic at all levels, and studies and research reports outside the academic institutions.

As examples of fresh work, new ideas and current developments, obviously these materials must be scanned by the serious student of librarianship. The delay between the completion of a piece of research and the general implementation of its findings may well be years, and to wait for separately published articles or monographs resulting from research involves carelessly ignoring some vital work simply because its form is different. Thus research literature needs to be examined both as an indication of current activity – research in progress – and as a historical body of material much of which has not appeared in any published version.

Access to this material has been a problem; universities lock it away and produce it reluctantly. In the United Kingdom the British Library Document Supply Centre has worked hard to obtain copies of theses, and to secure permission to lend them. In recent years publishers of microforms have moved into this field and made it possible to buy copies of research material, either on microfilm or in hard photographic copy in response to individual demands. Problems of identifying what is available and the prices charged ensure that this is a relatively small market.

The historical position can be considered first; here there is little non-academic work, since research activity outside the academic environment is a modern departure, so the material for which we are looking can be traced through the thesis and dissertation control services. The most important service is the American *Dissertation Abstracts International* compiled by University Microfilms and available from 1938. This lists doctoral dissertations with summaries and information on obtaining microfilm copies. An extension of this service has been the data base DATRIX II, which is the basis of *Comprehensive Dissertation Index 1861-1972* with supplements. Volume 31 of this Index – *Communications and the Arts* – includes library and information science, listed in an alphabetical sequence of keywords. Similar general coverage for the United Kingdom is provided by the Aslib *Index to Theses*, which began publication in 1950, and now includes higher degrees awarded in polytechnics and colleges by the Council for National Academic Awards as well as those awarded by universities; from 1986 abstracts are given for each entry, which greatly enhances the service. The historical extension of this is the *Retrospective Index to Theses of Great Britain and Ireland 1716-1950* edited by Roger Bilboul and published in five volumes by the Clio Press (1976).

Of more immediate relevance to our subject areas are a number of specialized guides. For North American work the most useful title is *Library Science Dissertations 1925-1972*, compiled by Gail A.

Schlater and Dennis Thomison (Libraries Unlimited, 1974), and a second volume covering 1973–1981 (Libraries Unlimited, 1982). Material is arranged year by year, annotations are given to indicate purpose, procedure and findings, and there are author and subject indexes. These two cumulations are now updated in section three: *abstracts of library science dissertations* of the new *Library Science Annual* (Libraries Unlimited) discussed in Chapter 10. The years 1925–1960 are also covered by *Library Science Dissertations*, compiled by N. M. Cohen, B. Denison and J. C. Boehlert and published in 1963 by the US Office of Health, Education and Welfare. This was reissued by Gregg Press in 1972.

University Microfilms have produced two guides: in 1975 C. H. Davis compiled *Doctoral Dissertations in Library Science: titles accepted by accredited library schools* covering the years 1930–1975, and this was extended in a volume of the same title published in 1981.

Work at master's degree level is recorded in three compilations by Shirley Magnotti: the first is *Masters Degrees in Library Science 1960–1969* (Whitson, Troy, New York, 1975), with supplementary volumes covering the years 1970–1974 (1976), and 1974–1979 (1982). The main British equivalent is *Library and Information Studies in the United Kingdom and Ireland, 1950–1974: an index to theses* edited by Peter J. Taylor of the Aslib Research Department (Aslib, 1976). This index is arranged year by year, with author and subject indexes. There are no annotations. Theses submitted to the Library Association are listed with abstracts in L. J. Taylor's *FLA theses: abstracts of all these accepted for the Fellowship of the Library Association from 1964* (British Library, 1979). Individual schools have also produced their own lists – for example, the *Catalogue of theses, dissertations and projects* from the University of Loughborough DLIS (1983).

The more vital area to the general user of librarianship literature is the determination of what research is currently in progress, what up-to-date reports are available, and to whom queries for more information can be addressed. In a profession moving rapidly into new areas of development, an accurate picture of what is being done, and where, can save the time and cost of duplicating research, and consequently great attention should be paid to the investigation of research in progress.

There have been international moves to co-ordinate and control research in librarianship and information science: after uncertain beginnings various worldwide projects have joined forces and one scheme is now emerging which has a chance of reasonable success. From 1973 Unesco produced *UNISIST Newsletter*, reporting on 'aspects of the development and implementation of a world-wide programme of scientific and technical information (UNISIST) and related activities'. A year earlier Unesco had also sponsored the foundation of ISORID: the International System on Research in Documentation. The aim of this was to 'collect, organise, analyse and disseminate information on research activities in the field of documentation, libraries and archives'. The activities of ISORID were reported in *Bibliography, Documentation, Terminology* from 1973 onwards; each country had a designated National Information Transfer Centre, and information appeared on new centres, reports received, and new projects. Various services were offered including a current awareness service, computer-based searches, and the provision of copies of reports. *Bibliography, Documentation Terminology* ceased publication at the end of 1978, and the ISORID section combined with the *UNISIST Newsletter* to form a new serial: *General Information Programme – Unisist Newsletter*.

This quarterly *Newsletter* reports on the UNISIST programme, activities of member states on the main scheme and all the manifold sub-branches of the Unesco General Information Programme. It is published in English, Arabic, French, Russian and Spanish. The cover of a recent issue (Figure 8.1) shows the worldwide nature of its work and the scope of its subject coverage. The Programme is making an enormous effort to control the work of third-world countries, and co-ordinate this with other research in progress. The scale of the task and the limits on finance pose huge problems: as a concept it is outstanding, but the mechanics of its achievement may prove unworkable. The bulk of the work on ISORID is now carried out by International Federation for Documentation (FID); its publication *R & D Projects in Documentation and Librarianship* now carries information on projects reported to ISORID, and FID has reached an agreement with Unesco to eliminate duplication, and provides services in support of ISORID. FID has also published a looseleaf *ISORID Directory of Institutional and Individual Activities* (1980), and is willing to provide information from its files to researchers wishing to discover any reported work in a given area. The opening page of *R & D Projects* gives a column of information on FID's role in ISORID (Figure 8.2).

In most countries it is the role of the professional association or the national library to co-ordinate research activity; at present, for example, the British position is particularly easy to understand. The British Library has established a Research and Development Department to encourage and support library and information research, including development work and practical applications. The Department is small, but has considerable funds at its disposal to award in grants for projects. A special emphasis is placed on the dissemination of results; the report of every project is listed in the Department's publications list, and many are published by the body that actually carried out the work. All reports, whether published or not, are available in microfiche copies from the British Library Document Supply Centre. In addition to a general listing, the Department also produces specialized lists. The Department also supports a number of research centres, based usually in academic institutions, each with an information officer, to collect and disseminate material in their subject: automation, catalogue research, reprography and user education are amongst the topics so far covered.

The Department's main regular publication is the *Research and Development Newsletter*, which gives details of grants and contracts, the availability of new reports with an abstract, and many announcements on research activity in progress and further developments of completed work.

The British Library, from its Document Supply Centre base, also produces annually *Current Research in Britain* (CRIB). This appears in four volumes: physical sciences, biological sciences, social sciences, and humanities. Data are collected from participating institutions on a voluntary basis, and may therefore be incomplete; projects are at post-doctoral level in some fields, higher master's in others. The main division within each volume is by broad subject: each volume carries index references to *libraries* and various divisions of the term *information* and a wide variety of relevant research taking place sometimes in unexpected locations can thus be traced.

The principal tool for investigation in our subject areas is *Current Research in Library and Information Science* (CRILIS), published quarterly by the Library Association from 1983. Its forerunners were *RADIALS Bulletin* (1978–1982) and the Register of Research contained in the Association's *Yearbook* (1968–1973).

FIGURE 8.1

ISSN 0379 - 2218

General Information Programme

Unisist Newsletter

Vol. 14, No. 1, 1986

Unesco

FIGURE 8.2

F I D
international federation
for documentation
Founded September 1895

R&D PROJECTS
IN DOCUMENTATION AND LIBRARIANSHIP

ISSN 0301-4436

Volume 16, Issue 2

March/April 1986

ISORID

INTERNATIONAL INFORMATION SYSTEM ON

RESEARCH IN DOCUMENTATION

The International Information System on Research in
Documentation (ISORID) established by UNESCO in cooperation with FID, is charged with collecting, organizing,
analyzing, storing and diffusing information on research
and development in the fields of information, documentation, libraries and archival records management.
    In order to achieve the objectives of ISORID more
effectively the following policy has been adopted and
approved by the Intergovernmental Council for the
General Information Programme of UNESCO:
- the extension of cooperation with the FID with a view
  to avoiding the duplication of activities between
  FID and UNESCO;
- the extension of ISORID by adding Member States which
  do not yet participate and by the inclusion in the
  system of information on research in the archive
  field;
- the improvement of the system's functioning in order

AT/A/4187
Vocational training; Artificial intelligence;
Content analysis; Terminology

*Development of an Expert System for Vocational Trai-
ning on a Terminological Basis*
    The aim of this project is to present information of
CEDEFOP on the state of the art in the fields of
terminology, documentation and artificial intelligence, in order to find appropriate solutions
for problems of multilingualism and information
science. The report should also include the topics
of the ESPRIT and FAST programmes of the EEC. The
methods applied include concept and content analysis.
1984-1985
Helmut Feiber, Wolfgang Nedobity, Christian Galinski,
International Information Centre for Terminology,
Austrian Standards Institute, P.O. Box 130, A-1021
.Vienna, Austria
.Sponsor: CEDEFOP - European Centre for the Development
of Vocational Training
Cost: ATS 400.000

ment covers the following points:

(a) all information on research is to be sent directly to FID;

(b) FID will assign descriptors to this information using the UNESCO *Thesaurus*;

(c) all relevant information received will be published by FID in its periodical bulletin *R & D Projects in Documentation and Librarianship*.

Published reports are also requested and should be sent to FID as well.

As mentioned above, projects published in *R & D Projects* are for the most part limited to those received by questionnaire. It is not the intent of *R & D Projects in Documentation and Librarianship* to reprint information on projects already published in established directories.

It is the intent of *R & D Projects* though to regularly include also information on publications which are devoted in part or totally to publishing data on research and development projects in librarianship, documentation, information science, and archival records management as well as related fields. The entries for these publications are assigned descriptors and included in the FID research referral services file.

Information on planned, on-going, and recently completed projects as well as information on published reports and directories of research in the fields is invited for inclusion in *R & D Projects*.

The FID research referral service is a manual file of information by subject and location on several thousand research projects collected since 1971. The main purpose of this system is to provide referrals to persons or organizations undertaking research in a given area, although other services may be provided on request.

Address all queries on the ISORID and the research referral service to FID at the address below.

The Development of Library and Information Services in Fiji

This thesis examined the influence of the economic, political and social factors on the development of various types of library and information services in Fiji. Education and training and the role of the local library association are also discussed.

1980-1982

Harry Singh, Department of School of Librarianship, Gippsland Institute of Advanced Education, Switchback Road, Churchill, Victoria 3842, Australia

AU/B/4189

Colonialism; History; History of libraries; Australia

The Diffusion of Useful Knowledge: Mechanics' Institute in Nineteenth Century Victoria

This project (Master of Arts thesis) traced the development of Victorian Mechanics' Institutes by first considering the fortunes of similar institutions in Great Britain. In the following chapters the establishment, objectives and problems of a number of institutes in colonial Victoria are analyzed. The characteristic functional areas of the institutes: the libraries, classes, museums are treated in detail. Similarly attention is given to the local contexts which influenced their development, as well as the major ideological elements which continued to influence the activities of the founders and committees. In addition, the author uses subscription lists and annual reports to assess the social and economic characteristics of the membership.

1982

Mark Richard Askew, 112 Scotchmer Street, North Fitzroy, Victoria 3068, Australia

R & D Projects in Documentation and Librarianship (FID Publication 485) is published bimonthly by the General Secretariat of the International Federation for Documentation (FID) with the financial assistance of UNESCO and is an integral part of the UNESCO International Information System on Research in Documentation (ISORID). Subscriptions: f 85,00 per year. FID, P.O. Box 90402, 2509 LK The Hague, Netherlands.

FIGURE 8.3

N/Q ORGANISATION AND ADMINISTRATION
(Continued)

Nbmf'w—Planning. County libraries. Peterborough (Canada)   86/3/18

Feasibility study into larger units of library service (Peterborough County)

Research worker(s): Peter Barnard Associates. *Duration:* 1985 – 1986. *Financial support:* Ontario Ministry of Citizenship and Culture – Larger Units of Public Library Service Feasibility Study Program – $25 000.

The study will investigate the possibility of establishing more union libraries or a county library system in the county. Peter Barnard Associates will assess the economic advantages of increased co-operation between libraries and the resulting impact on service levels. A budget forecast will be prepared showing scenarios including: the status quo; development of union libraries; and the establishment of a county library system. A local study committee has been appointed to help guide the project.

Nbmf'w—Planning. County libraries. Prescott and Russell (Canada)   86/3/19

Feasibility study into larger units of library service (United Counties of Prescott and Russell).

Research worker(s): J. L. Richards & Associates. *Duration:* 1985 – 1986. *Financial support:* Ontario Ministry of Citizenship and Culture – Larger Units of Public Library Service Feasibility Study Program – $25 000.

This study will investigate the possibility of establishing a county library system in the United Counties of Prescott and Russell.

Nj/x—ADMINISTRATION (MANAGEMENT)

Ntt & Nj—Budgets. Cuts. And Management. Academic libraries. Canada. Surveys   86/3/20

Management of retrenchment in Canadian academic research libraries.

Research worker(s): Laurent-G. Denis (Dr), Ethel Auster (Dr), Terry Germanson, Carol Coughlin at University of Toronto; Faculty of Library and Information Science. *Duration:* 1983 – 1986.

Pj/jo—PROFESSIONAL STAFF (Continued)

Branch.

Using data from the SLIS [School of Library and Information Science] Career Path Survey which was carried out in 1984 with a Faculty-Student grant, this project will define the personal and professional correlates of success in the library field in Canada. What are successful librarians like? Are they particularly aggresive or motivated? Do they have superior communicative skills? Have they always aspired to a library career? Did they have a role model or preceptor? Are there gender, language, or regional related differences? In short, what makes the successful librarian different? How does he/she diverge from certain typical patterns discovered in the SLIS Career Path Survey data? *Further information:* J. Tague.

Q/Qu—BUILDINGS AND EQUIPMENT

Q/QuAw—*Viewpont of Students.* Polytechnic libraries. Newcastle upon Tyne Polytechnic Library in-house research programme   86/3/23

Students' opinions of the library study environment.

Research worker(s): Liz McDowell (Research and Planning Librarian), Ian Winship (Faculty Librarian) at Newcastle upon Tyne Polytechnic; Library. *Duration:* March 1986 – July 1986. *Financial support:* Newcastle Polytechnic.

A questionnaire survey is being undertaken to discover student views on the physical aspects of the library environment. The questionnaire covers aspects such as seating arrangements (individual vs large tables); quietness and noise; the need for group work facilities; refreshment facilities. The questionnaires are being distributed by lecturers and completed during staff time so that a high response rate is expected. The results will be used in considering modifications to the library environment. *Further information:* Liz McDowell.

R/S—READER SERVICES

RaFv &—Public libraries. Surrey County Library (UK).   86/3/24 plexity and stratification are probed in these studies. In addition, the study seeks to discover how chief library administrators have implemented changes necessitated by declining resources; what has happened to managers at various levels of the organisation and to general librarians, and how these changes relate to the structural characteristics of the organisations and to the chief executive's perception of his/her implementation of decline. Data will be gathered by questionnaire sent to all professional personnel in libraries which are members of the Canadian Association of Research Libraries, and by in-depth interviews with chief librarians and a sample of personnel at other management levels. *Further information:* L.-G. Denis.

P—STAFF

PehNjGip—Staff time. Management. Polytechnic libraries. **86/3/21**
Newcastle upon Tyne Polytechnic Library, UK
+ Allocation of staff time.

Research worker(s): Liz McDowell (Research and Planning Librarian) at Newcastle upon Tyne Polytechnic; Library. *Duration:* May 1985 – December 1985. *Financial support:* Newcastle upon Tyne Polytechnic.

Data was collected on the use of staff time, using, library staff's own estimates. It is realised that these can be inaccurate but it is hoped that with the broad categories of activity used, eg. cataloguing, collection management, book acquisitions, this is not too serious a problem. The staff time and costs devoted to particular activities have been calculated. Comparisons have been made with a previous study in 1980 to indicate changes which have taken place and an assessment has been made of the use of staff at appropriate grades for particular activities. *Reference(s):* Newcastle upon Tyne Polytechnic Library: *Allocation of staff 1985* Planning and Research Note No. 64. [Internal report]. *Further information:* Liz McDowell.

Pj/jo—PROFESSIONAL STAFF

Pjk &—Chief librarians. Careers development. Canada. **86/3/22**
Surveys
Pathways to success: personal characteristics and career paths of the chief administrators of large Canadian libraries.

Research worker(s): Jean Tague (Dr), Roma M. Harris (Dr) at University of Western Ontario; School of Library and Information Science. *Duration:* 1986. *Financial support:* Ontario Minstry of Citizenship and Culture, Libraries and Community Information

1986 – continuing.

A review team has been established to evaluate all aspects of library provision within defined catchment areas. The aims are to identify standards of provision and service performance and to enable services and resources to be tailored accurately to meet the demands of each catchment community. A variety of research techniques are being used and developed in aspects of market research, catchment analysis and data collection. Projects include geographical and socio-economic analysis of users, user surveys of various types, research into trends of use by new borrowers, investigations into lapsed use, analysis of stock and stock use, and assessments of performance measures. The research will continue for three years, but some examples of surveys and data collection are already available. *Further information:* Graham Combe.

RaHyk—To Children. Denmark. **86/3/25**
An investigation into the practices of conveying information, culture and literature in children's libraries with a view to developing methods for such practices, especially targeted at fictional literature.

Research worker(s): Marianne Hjort-Lorenzen (Project Head, 24 Jernbanegade contact address: Frederikssund Library, DK-3600 Frederikssund, Denmark), Eva Glistrup (Adviser), Dorte Skot-Hansen (Adviser), Sus Rostrup (Adviser), Jens Thorhauge (Adviser) at State Inspection of Public Libraries Copenhagen. *Duration:* 1 October 1984 – 1 January 1987. *Financial support:* The Public Libraries' Special Grants Scheme administered within the framework of the Danish Public Libraries Act – D.kr. 453 500.

The project aims to refine children's library-operated practices of conveying information, culture and literature. The historical background and the current situation relating to this problem area are analysed and the currnt trends in conveying practices are isolated and identified as part of the basis of the envisaged lines of development and progress of the project. The main emphasis is placed on the conveying of literature to children and adults frequenting the children's and young people's departments in public libraries. The intention is to develop methods to be applied in the practical conveying work. The methods should emanate from/be based on the requirements made by children and adults of the conveying practices in relation to their daily lives and the needs and wishes that stem from their everyday situation. Hence, an essential requirement to be met by the methods, is that they are dynamic in nature. The project results should contribute to the development of more differentiated and methodical conveying practices in children's and young people's departments. The practices aimed at should be more variable in relation to current times and to the users. This implies that the books will be used in a more differentiated and

FIGURE 8.4

CRILIS is a part of the FID Research Referral Service, and unlike its predecessors is international in coverage; contributions are received from 44 countries and the United Nations and European Economic Community. About 1,300 items are listed each year.

A wide definition of research is taken; included in it are studies, surveys, evaluated innovations, British Standards, and in-house or action-research from practising professionals as well as academic-type research. In this last category doctoral, post-doctoral and research staff work is included; sub-doctoral theses and dissertations are listed separately under the name of the institution, but no information is given other than title and items are not included in the indexes.

CRILIS appears four times per year; parts 1–3 contain only new work, while part 4 is cumulative and provides an updated entry for all current projects and those completed in the last year. In 1986 it became possible to search *CRILIS* via DIALOG.

The arrangement of entries in the main sequence is in classified order using the CRG classification scheme also seen in *Library and Information Science Abstracts* (LISA). The specimen page (Figure 8.3) shows the layout: each entry is filed by the alphabetical *CRG* number, with an explanation of that number expressed in key terms. There is a running number for each entry, using the form year/issue number/item number. The title of the research project is given, the names of the research workers, the duration of the project and the financial sponsor. For academic work, the qualification sought is also given. A description of the project is provided by the researchers, and this concludes with the name of a contact for further information.

On black-edged pages at the end of each issue there are two indexes; the first is a name index featuring names of individuals and corporate bodies, and from 1986 onwards entries by names of countries. Secondly, there is an alphabetical subject index (for a specimen page see Figure 8.4), which includes references to preferred terms and related headings. Names of countries, subdivided by topic, are indexed here as well as in the name index. The numbers given in the index refer to the running number of the entries in each year.

Additionally the Library Association is publishing hard-back annual cumulated versions of *CRILIS*: *Current research in the information profession 1984/85, 1985/86* and *1986/87* have so far appeared.

CABLIS, the Bulletin produced by the British Library/Library Association Library, discussed more fully in Chapter 10, includes a selection of brief abstracts headed 'Notes on research reports', and also gives abstracts of theses in relevant subject fields added to the stock of the Library. Such material is also fully covered by *LISA*, and *Library Literature* similarly indexes US dissertations and theses.

Library and Information Research News, published quarterly by the Library and Information Research Group (affiliated to the Library Association) contains discussions of UK research papers, reviews of reports, and surveys of current activity.

Reviews of current research in North America are to be found in two journals: *Journal of Education for Librarianship and Information Science* includes a regular feature 'research record' which briefly reviews important new theses, and lists doctoral dissertation topics accepted. *Library and Information Science Research* journal has a 'dissertation review' section; this usually discusses two or three pieces of work only.

Further controls on research literature are usually provided by national library associations, which will probably attempt to list and collect all new dissertations and theses at doctoral level or abve. Work within individual Schools of Librarianship is usually recorded in some kind of research bulletin. Much of the lower-level work may not be generally available, but the bulletins should reveal the names of researchers and supervisors who could be contacted for further information if a topic of particular interest is mentioned.

9   Additional sources, and routes to further information

To attempt to document all possible sources of information in librarianship and information science would be a purposeless task; the preceding chapters have outlined the chief sources, and given hints on tracing further information. It is the intention of this chapter to add some other widely-known secondary sources, to discuss certain areas which have not been treated fully, and to indicate further likely paths to information for those who cannot trace their requirements adequately in the available published sources. Information is presented here under a series of subheadings.

Biography: Biographical information on librarians and information officers is not a well-covered topic; for the UK and old Commonwealth countries the only comprehensive source is *Who's who in librarianship and information science*, edited by T. Landau, (2nd ed., Abelard-Schuman, 1972) which includes entries on an inconsistent and haphazard basis, and gives only basic information on education, appointments and publications. Many of those included are now retired, and obviously several now prominent names did not wish to be included when the volume was being compiled. A second international source, with a strong US bias, is the *ALA World Encyclopedia of Library and Information Services*, 2nd. ed. (discussed in an earlier chapter), which includes biographical sections on prominent figures worldwide. A specialized US source is the *Dictionary of American Library Biography* edited by B.S. Wynar (Libraries Unlimited, 1978), which has substantial entries for more than 300 figures. Unlike the previous two works, Wynar includes only those who were deceased at the time of compilation and the volume is therefore only of use historically, not for gleaning information on current personalities in the profession. The American Library Association published in 1982 *Who's who in library and information services*, edited by Joel M. Lee, which further extends the coverage of United States professionals.

Government publications: Major abstracting and indexing services discussed in a previous chapter will cover the reports and other publications which emanate from government agencies. In the UK the normal general alerting services of HMSO daily, monthly and annual lists will provide current information on newer publications. The HMSO *Sectional List No. 2*, listing publications of the Department of Education and Science and re-issued at regular intervals, includes a section on the library service which features important reports, miscellaneous government reports and proceedings of committees, and publications in the *Library Information Series* which are often the result of work undertaken for the Library and Information Services Council.

In the same *List* are reports in other areas relevant to our fields, including science and research, and higher and further education.

For US government activity a number of current sources are available in addition to the general *Monthly Catalog*; relevant reports are noted in several periodicals, such as *Library Resources and Technical Services, College and Research Libraries, Information Hotline*, and *Information Retrieval and Library Automation Letter*. The US Department of Commerce National Technical Information Service (NTIS) produces a weekly abstract newsletter *Library and information sciences* (Figure 9.1) which covers government and other reports. An annual subject index to this newsletter appears each January. Other countries have a variety of general and specialized services to control government publications; for specific requirements the relevant sections of A. J. Walford's *Guide to reference materials*, volume 3 (4th ed., Library Association, 1986) and E. P. Sheehy's *Guide to reference books* (10th ed., ALA, 1987) should be checked.

Library law: The law relating to library services is well documented in the UK and USA; for other countries the professional associations should be consulted for current information. In the UK, L. J. Talylor's *Librarian's Handbook* vol. 1 (Library Association, 1976) and vol. 2 (Library Association, 1980) provides the texts of current legislative documents, and represents the most convenient method of discovering relevant documents and reading them in their entirety. For the public library sector A. R. Hewitt's *Public library law* (5th ed.,

Association of Assistant Librarians, 1975) comprises a valuable exposition and commentary; it is thoroughly indexed.

The US situation is covered by A. Ladenson's *American library law* (5th ed., ALA, 1983): this provides full details of current federal and state legislation.

Standards: Standards organizations have a valuable but limited relevance to the study of librarianship and information science; the British Standards Institution's chief importance here is their revision and production of the English edition of the Universal Decimal Classification. Details of new schedules, amendments and revisions are recorded each month in *BSI News,* and the current *BSI Yearbook* provides full details of all available schedules, auxiliary tables, amendments and the abridged edition. The International Standards Organisation has also produced relevant items.

Standards for library provision were listed by F. N. Withers in *Standards for library service* (Unesco, 1970), now rather out of date for developed countries but still a good starting point for third-world countries, where adoption of standards is less rapid. Withers reproduced standards for all types of library, and for each type arranged his material by country. For the current UK position, the full texts of relevant standards are reproduced in the two volumes of L. J. Taylor's *Librarian's Handbook* (cited above); for other countries, the professional association is the most likely source of complete and up-to-date information.

Statistics: The fullest international source of statistical information on libraries is the *Unesco Statistical Yearbook* (Unesco, annual). The section relating to libraries records for each country the number of libraries, number of volumes and length of shelving within six categories of collections – national, higher education, school, special, public and 'non-specialised'. Information given, however, is frequently several years out of date; a number of tables analyse book production, translations, periodicals and newspapers. For the British position, Alan MacDougall's *Statistical series in library and information services* (Elsevier, 1985) surveys available statistical series, evaluates their relevance, and points to gaps and shortcomings.

Once again here L. J. Taylor's *Librarian's Handbook* (cited above) provides British information, and the Chartered Institute of Public

FIGURE 9.1

NTIS

Library & Information Sciences

AN ABSTRACT NEWSLETTER

Tuesday, September 23, 1986
Volume 86, Number 38
PLEASE SEE PRICE SCHEDULE ON BACK COVER

PB86-908838

COVERING

Operations & planning

Information systems

Marketing & user services

Personnel

Reference materials

22304-5110.

OPERATIONS & PLANNING

International Corporation), 3900 Wheeler Ave., Alexandria, VA 22304-5110.
ED-266 793   Not available NTIS

Eight articles in this Spring 1985 issue of The Bookmark focus on young adult library services. In addition to these thematic articles, an introduction and three reports are presented. The issue contains: (1) 'In Perspective' (E. J. Josey); (2) 'Young Adult Literature in the 1980's--Awesome' (Ellin Chu); (3) 'Young Adult Services' Public Relations and Promotion' (Carol Dratch-Kovler); (4) 'Microcomputers and Young Adults' (Barbara Newmark-Kruger); (5) 'Library Service to Rural Youth' (Joanne Burr); (6) 'Books on Personal Development for Teenagers' (Lydia LaFleur); (7) 'Strengthening Young Adult Work with the New Young Adult Standards' (Rhonna A. Goodman); (8) 'Would Teens Run Riot in the Library - Youth Participation in Public Libraries' (Ristiina Wigg); (9) 'Input and Output: The Functioning of a Youth Advisory Council' (Suzanne M. Ponzini and Sheldon L. Tarakan); (10) 'Report to the Board of Regents Cultural Education Committee by the Regents Advisory Council on Libraries, May 23, 1985' (Carol Kearney); (11) 'Survey of Public Library Services for Deaf People' (Karen Matthews); and (12) 'Summary and Evaluation of New York State LSCA (Library Services and Construction Act) Program, FY 1983.' (THC).

38,002-688
Guide to the Archives of International Organizations. Part 3.
A. W. Mabbs.
United Nations Educational, Scientific and Cultural Organization, Paris (France). General Information Programme. Aug 85, 47p PGI-85/WS/19 For Parts 1 and 2 of this guide, see ED 188 592 and IR 051 412. Available from ERIC Document Reproduction Service (Computer Microfilm International Corporation), 3900 Wheeler Ave., Alexandria, VA

categories. Intergovernmental organizations created before 1950 and non-governmental organizations with category A, B, or C relationships with Unesco and created before 1950. Responses were received from 64 organizations (26% of those polled); the entries are arranged alphabetically by title of the organization and most include: postal address, telephone number, year of founding, description of archives, access information, and research facilities. The amount of detail and clarity of description of each organization's archives varies considerably from entry to entry. The questionnaire (Appendix A) was designed to provide the opportunity for organizations with extensive and well-organized archives to give precise and detailed information, while enabling others to provide only a few basic facts if they preferred. A list of the 246 organizations to which the questionnaire was sent is appended. (THC).

38,003-688
Library Services to Special Needs Populations in Wisconsin, 1975-1984.
F. de Usabel, and D. W. Johnson.
Wisconsin State Dept. of Public Instruction, Madison. Div. of Library Service. Jan 86, 85p BULL-6263 Available from ERIC Document Reproduction Service (Computer Microfilm International Corporation), 3900 Wheeler Ave., Alexandria, VA 22304-5110.
ED-266 795   Not available NTIS

The final product of the Wisconsin Special Users Needs Assessment project initiated in the summer of 1984, this report outlines how library systems have worked with hard-to-reach and underserved populations over the past 10 years. The document is divided into three parts. Based on a review of the systems' annual plans and evaluations for the past decade, the first section is a narrative profile of each library system's program for its users with special needs and in-

Finance and Accountancy publish annually *Public Library Statistics* detailing all categories of expenditure by public authorities. The Canadian and American Library Associations have published relevant documents, and further American statistics can be traced in the *Bowker Annual of Library and Book Trade Information* (Bowker, annual) and in *Library Science Annual* (Libraries Unlimited, annual) both of which are further discussed in Chapter 10.

Professional education: Professional education and training is a large-scale, complex business in the UK, several Commonwealth countries, and the USA. For the UK and USA the Library Association and American Library Association will provide full details of qualifications, educational requirements and schools. This is true also of Canada, Australia, New Zealand, India and South Africa. For most other countries the range of courses, numbers of schools and qualifications awarded are more limited in scale and scope. The best guide here is the *International Guide to library and information science education*, edited by J.R. Fang and P. Nauta (K.G. Saur, for IFLA, 1985); this volume is a tremendous achievement, covering over 500 courses in one hundred countries. The arrangement is in a standard format by country, and adequately indexed.

Awards, grants and research funds: Gale Research Inc. publishes a two-volume compendium of *Awards, honors and prizes* (6th ed., 1985). The subject index to this shows library science and many related headings, and a large number of awards are listed applicable to our fields. For research funds it is difficult to trace a source of information; within each country the professional association or national library is the most likely channel for research activity. In addition to help they may offer, general guides to research funding will be of assistance. In a developing field, it is frequently a useful ploy to examine in *CRILIS* and similar publications the sources which research projects show as their sponsors. Depending on the nature of the research, social science or scientific foundations may be interested in widening their traditional fields and should always be approached for advice and opinion.

Routes to further information

The preceding chapters of this book have dealt with information as it exists in a published form; in the opening sections we noted that publication of a monograph title or a single volume reference work might take two years from initial preparation to final appearance. For larger, multi-volume encyclopedias the time taken is likely to exceed that. Indexes and abstracts record data published in books and in periodicals; although serial literature may be faster to appear than monographs, nevertheless the time taken in writing, submission of papers to referees, and delay before publication, perhaps of a quarterly issue, still places a gap of several months between writing and publication. Indexes and abstracts may themselves impose a further delay between the publication of a piece of work and its appearance in their pages.

In a practical context, a librarian who is contemplating purchasing new equipment, adopting a new cataloguing system, regrading staff or restructuring a service wants for a decision information which is immediately current and relevant. Activities of the weeks and months just passed are more likely to hold clues to the best course of action than information on work done even one year ago.

To ensure that such current information can be found requires two approaches; the first of these is to be generally well-informed and up to date in the relevant field – this will demand familiarity with the most important monographs on the topic, regular scanning of key journals, and checking abstracts and indexes as they appear. This approach is more fully explored in the following chapter, which is concerned with keeping up to date with new developments either generally in our fields or on particular topics.

The second required approach to ensure current information is to desert the literature and direct enquiries to those organizations which collect and disseminate information in the area in question.

Professional associations: The role of the professional associations is crucial; they are at the centre of national activity in the profession, and have a co-ordinating role if not an active role in most aspects of professional life. Generally they run a library service or information department which will collect relevant material and make it available to enquirers. Where specialized branches or separate groups exist to cover smaller fields of work or geographical divisions, the central association will be able to provide addresses and names of contacts.

The initial source of information will be the association's directory; in the United Kingdom the Library Association annually publishes a *Yearbook* which gives details of the headquarters services, the senior staff, the details of the organization, its council and committees, and details of the branches, groups and sections of the Association with names of the personnel on their controlling committees. The *Yearbook* also gives information on library facilities at the headquarters, and details of awards and research grants, as well as the full list of personal and institutional members.

The American Library Association similarly produces an annual *Handbook of Organisation and Membership Directory* which describes the organization, its policies and aims, and gives details of council and committees, divisions, round tables, and chapters. Information on headquarters services is provided and a series of appendices give full texts of key documents and details of membership services. The Canadian Library Association publishes the *Canadian Library Handbook* (3rd ed., 1983) which gives details of some 150 associations and organizations.

Internationally, there is an annual *Directory* of members of the International Federation of Library Associations and Institutions (IFLA), which gives details of the headquarters secretariat and services, regional offices and staff, and full lists of the members of each of the main committees, divisions, sections, and round tables.

The fullest compendium of international activity is J.R. Fang and A.H. Songe's *International Guide to Library, Archival and Information Science Associations* (2nd ed., Bowker, 1980). The *Guide* is in two sections: the first relates to international associations, the second to national associations arranged by country. Each entry gives the official name of the association, an acronym if any is used, and an English translation where necessary. Current addresses are provided, names of the executive officers and senior staff, and a statement of the main fields of interest. Further information given includes the date of foundation, objectives, structure, financial organization, types of membership and the total number, details of publications, principal activities, and a bibliography to illustrate aspects of the association's work.

There are entries under a very large number of countries, and for developed countries where there are many organizations full details of each are given to the pattern outlined above; for the United States, for example, details of 73 associations are given, from leading organizations such as ALA and ASIS, through the main specialist groups – SLA, MLA, ACRL for instance – to small and highly specialized associations. National organizations only are included; smaller regional groups, State associations and the like, are not a part of the *Guide*.

Several useful appendices are provided, including an alphabetical list of the official journals and newsletters of the associations described. The *Guide* provides an excellent introduction to the range of activities in any country, and for comparative work is the obvious starting point for identifying and locating relevant national organizations.

Publishers: Professional associations' publishing departments and commercial publishers should be regarded as indicators of current interests and activities; most publishers announce new titles months ahead of publication, and the 'Cataloguing in Publication' system now gives preliminary details of forthcoming titles in national bibliographies with usually reliable anticipated publication dates. Not only does this information demonstrate which areas of professional activity are reckoned the most popular, but much search time can be saved if a forthcoming title from a reputable publisher is likely to cover a sought topic. A new monograph should represent a distillation of current practice, and if one is scheduled to appear it may render redundant a time-consuming literature and information search.

Publishing acitivity in library and information science is in the hands only of a few well-known firms, academic institutions, and professional associations. All these bodies produce catalogues and publicity material which should be scanned to reveal the information we have suggested.

Audio-visual producers: Like publishers, producers of audio-visual packages are anxious to give advance information to their market; bibliographical control of such material is far less satisfactory than that of conventional publishing, and the role of the producer's own publicity may therefore be more important. Joseph W. Palmer surveys this field thoroughly; his article identifies the most important items and producers, and appends valuable lists of selection aids, and of producers and distributors (Palmer, 1979). Over 100 programmes produced for use in teaching librarianship or information work, or used in staff training, are listed in *Librarianship: a select audiovisual resource list* (British Universities Film & Video Council and Aslib Audiovisual Group, 1985).

Equipment manufacturers: To obtain current information on new products and services the most reliable course will be to talk to those who have had experience of using the items in question. This is now made much easier by the existence of user groups for those employing similar systems, and by non-profit-making networks. In such cases the experience of users of products can be of value to point up potential areas of difficulty; conferences and seminars are also arranged by such groups to share their members' experiences.

Manufacturers themselves will of course be pleased to offer information; provided that prospective purchasers keep their critical instincts sharpened and know what they need to find out, they should feel no inhibition in asking for demonstrations and explanations. Exhibitions provide the opportunity to examine a range of equipment in a less formal setting than an arranged visit, and comparisons can readily be made between rival firms. Where exhibitions are held as part of professional conferences it is easier to find other participants who may have experience of the products on display and are prepared to discuss them.

It is unfortunate that few independent agencies exist to evaluate machinery and systems for purchaser; the Library Technology Centre at the Polytechnic of Central London offers demonstrations and arranges seminars, and can offer initial advice. Within a smaller field *CIMTECH* (the National Centre for Information Media and Technology) at Hatfield Polytechnic in the UK offers a useful series of reports evaluating micrographic hardware. These reports – identified by a TER code number (technical evaluation reports) – give full technical details of the machine, and impartially offer an opinion on its suitability for its intended job.

Libraries as sources: 1 – employer groups: For impartial infor-mation on products, and opinions on any aspect of professional affairs, the professional associations discussed above may offer assistance; however, more practical and sharper comments may come from those organizations representing practising librarians as employers rather than as a profession. Such organizations need not feel the same restraint on giving offence to other groups, can act independently of any parent organization, and can state their case forcibly to impress political authorities.

In the United Kingdom the *Circle of State Librarians,* the *Council of Polytechnic Librarians (COPOL)* and the *Standing Conference of National and University Libraries (SCONUL)* are examples of such employer groupings. Their policy statements can give the clearest guidance on current trends, and their newsletters convey a picture of the areas of work which they consider most important.

Libraries as sources: 2 – *employee groups*: Equally informative are the newsletters produced by library employees and employee organizations. These range from staff newsletters recording informal occurrences and social events, with occasional more serious contributions, to newsletters primarily designed to help in the training or professional development of staff; these latter especially provide basic, down-to-earth information on new policies and services, and indicate the successes and problems involved in new techniques or technology.

A second category of material comes from trade union sources; reports and newsletters issued by unions highlight the practical side of a developing service. The acceptability of new techniques and the implications of new technology on the workforce will be analysed, and provide an indication of the advantages and difficulties involved. In the UK the Library Association collects material on union activities and issues a newsletter – *LA Trade Union News* – which reports on cuts, regrading, staff structures, job sharing, new technology and salary claims. In the United States the most complete statement is the paper 'Union activities in US libraries' written by Claude J. Johns for the *Encyclopedia of Library and Information Science* (vol. 31, pp. 356–390) (seé chapter 5). This includes a substantial bibliography.

Libraries as sources: 3 – subject collections: The final tool available to the researcher is a library devoted to the subject fields required, providing facilities to browse and discover specialized information from a large stock. In the United States there are many libraries with extensive stock in librarianship and information science; these can best be traced through the volumes of the *Directory of Special Libraries and Information Centres* (9th ed., Gale Research, 1985). This *Directory* is now regularly updated by a periodic supplement *New Special*

Libraries. For subject access to library science collections, the *Subject Directory* volumes need to be scanned.

Also covering the United States and Canada is Lee Ash's *Subject Collections* (5th ed., Bowker, 1978) which has extensive listings of libraries with important collections in library science, information science and related fields. The *Research Centers Directory* (10th ed.: 1986, Gale Research, 1985) includes librarianship in its social science section, and can provide important clues to the locations of the larger research units and their supporting library and information resources. The whole North American library science collection network is neatly outlined by Joel M. Lee (1979), and Purcell and Schlachter (1984) have an extensive section of directories, arranged country by country, and State by State, within the United States (pp. 79–139). Further general information can be found in the *American Library Directory*, 39th ed. (Bowker, 1986) and the bimonthly *ALD* updating service. Internationally the *World Guide to Libraries*, 7th ed. (K. G. Saur, 1986) is the standard work.

In the United Kingdom provision of specialized collections is far more modest; in terms of large thorough stocks there are only two collections, the British Library/Library Association library at the Library Association headquarters, and the library at the College of Librarianship Wales. The *Aslib Directory* and the new *Shorter Aslib Directory* (Aslib, 1986) will expand on this.

This chapter can only offer hints for further work; librarianship and information science are such pervasive disciplines that no clear limit can be set beyond which information will not be found. The student or researcher needs always to think of the implications of the topic both within and outside the professional fields, and use sources discussed in this book together with other wider scanning to obtain a picture in perspective. The information in this chapter particularly must be regarded as no more than an indication of the types of material available and the routes that might be followed. Further likely approaches will emerge in discussion of updating sources in the following chapter.

10   Keeping up to date

Chapters in this book have so far examined the routes to information in librarianship and information science, and have described the means of gathering data on a required topic on a systematic basis. This chapter aims to identify the types of publication available that can provide a current awareness service to the librarian or information worker, either over the whole range of professional interest, or in a smaller area of concern. It is particularly true here that individuals may have their own preferred publications, and it is our intention to point out the various categories of material that should be sought and examined, rather than to list every conceivable item.

The chapter will begin by examining *state-of-the-art* type publications, then consider *newsletters, current awareness services* and *information contacts*. Finally we shall mention *directories and guides* and sources for *reviews of new publications*.

State-of-the-art: Whether for exploring a new area, or consolidating knowledge of a current interest, a number of fairly general publications exist which can provide an overall picture of present activity.

Over the last fifteen years Academic Press has published an annual series entitled *Advances in Librarianship*; each volume identifies a series of broad topics, and specialist authors contribute substantial pieces demonstrating the current situation in this field. The bias of the series is definitely North American, but has a more international relevance. Each volume begins with a note of the contents of previous volumes in the series, which is a quick ready reference to topics covered; obviously with a series such as this currency is vital, and material in many of the earlier volumes is now only of historic use. Each section carries extensive references, and there are thorough author and subject indexes.

A similar series, complementary in scope, is the *Annual Review of Information Science and Technology (ARIST)*; this has been produced since 1966, under the editorial control of the American Society for Information Science (ASIS). The publishers have changed over the years; currently it is issued by Knowledge Industry Publications Inc. *ARIST* also has a policy of selecting a number of topics for treatment in each volume, and no single topic is repeated annually. Each section is written by a specialist, and aims to discuss trends in that field, as well as to record the current position. References are appended to each section, and frequently record over 100 items – an extremely valuable source of further reading. *ARIST* overall is a scholarly work that has a reputation for providing an authoritative summary in its field; although North American in origin, it is international in its coverage.

Each volume has an index in dictionary form; for subject indexing, the terminology has been standardized, with *see* references, and the indexing is therefore by concept rather than by words. There are cross references to related headings. The index covers the bibliographies as well as the articles themselves, with page numbers for the former italicized. Although the value of information in *ARIST* is essentially its currency, a retrospective index is useful; a cumulative index was issued separately to volumes 1–7, but this is now superceded by a KWOC index to volumes 1–15, which appeared as the final part of volume 15. This index sorts on authors, titles and all content words.

Another North American series is the *Proceedings of the Clinic on Library Applications of Data Processing* published by the Graduate School of Library Science, University of Illinois. Each annual volume takes a theme of general interest in the field, for example 'the role of the library in an electronic society', 'problems and failures in library automation', and presents a series of papers by specialist authors. Some of these are devoted to specific topics, others are general reviews of the covered topics.

Information science is also well covered in the annual series *Progress in Communication Sciences* issued by Ablex Publishing Corporation, of which the first volume appeared in 1979. The purpose of the series is to provide authoritative reviews on information, information transfer, information systems, the uses and effects of communications, and the control and regulating of communications and information. Each volume includes ten or twelve review articles,

with good bibliographies. JAI Press publishes two useful series –
Advances in Library Administration and Organisation and *Advances in
Library Automation and Networking*, the latter of which commenced in
1986.

Another annual publication providing a wealth of current
information is the *Bowker Annual of Library and Book Trade
Information*; R.R. Bowker has been responsible for thirty-one editions
of this title, which has become established as one of the most useful
volumes to the librarian. Its coverage is primarily the traditional areas
of librarianship, and the book trade; information science receives scant
attention. However, in its covered area it is excellent. Each volume
begins with a brief series of reports selected from *Library Journal,
School Library Journal* and *Publishers' Weekly*, showing the situation
overall in the preceding year; there follow special reports on current
controversial topics, and information on federal agencies, federal
libraries, national associations, legislation, funding and grants.
Sections following provide news on education, salaries, research,
statistics and a number of international comparisons. There are lists of
those books which have received awards in the preceding year, and the
best seller titles. A directory section provides information for national,
State, provincial and regional professional associations, and book
trade organizations. *Bowker Annual* is of course North American in
orientation apart from certain comparative information, but is an
extraordinarily comprehensive source of current information – the
1986 volume containing 800 pages. The edition for 1981 contained a
five-year cumulative index referring directly to the volumes for 1977–
1981. All articles and charts which have appeared in those volumes are
indexed here, but not material from the directory sections. Previous
cumulative indexes appeared in the volumes for 1976, 1971 and 1965.

A useful though far briefer summary of the preceding year's
events is contained in the 'news in review' section of *Library Journal*
each January.

The American Library Association *Yearbook of Library and Information Services* provides a comprehensive annual survey of the preceding year's activities in the United States; it includes feature articles on
important topics, and reports and reviews of special events. The *Yearbook* is seen as an annual supplement to the second edition of the *World
Encyclopedia of Library and Information Services* and thus these two
titles together provide an excellent up-to-date review of the US scene.

An important new production is *Library Science Annual,* edited by Bohdan S. Wynar and published by Libraries Unlimited. The first volume covered 1985 and was published at the end of that year. Some 150 names are given as editorial contributors, both librarians and faculty staff, of whom six are Canadian and all others United States-based.

LSA consists of four sections; firstly, a set of essays each of 5,000–12,000 words in length, and offering a substantial review of an area: for example, database reviewing, the Canadian library press, information science in the 1980s. Each essay is supported by abundant references and is a state-of-the-art summary.

The second section is a review of recent professional books; the subject is split into useful categories, and each review (of 500–1,000 words) is signed, clearly indicates the reviewer's recommendation, and usually quotes locations of other reviews. Each item has a running number; 253 books were covered in the first volume.

Section three reviews periodicals, providing a historical and descriptive account of a selection of titles, with some evaluations and comparisons. Forty-two titles were examined in the 1985 volume.

The fourth part of *LSA* consists of abstracts of library science dissertations: 102 items are discussed, from 44 institutions, and the information is presented in a standard format, divided into various research categories. Finally, *LSA* includes an excellent and extensive index.

The secondary category of publishing that aims to record the current situation are textbook-type monographs that describe themselves as *readers, guides, handbooks, manuals* and *introductions.* These are written for a wider audience than library-school students, and should not be overlooked by practising librarians needing a survey of the situation in a given area. It is true as with all monographs that publication delays make the contents out of date on the day of issue, and the value of the work as a contemporary picture decreases as the months go by. Generally after two or three years such monographs must be used with great care as much information will have become incorrect.

The 'standard' texts in any particular area will change from year to year and to attempt to list current examples will serve no purpose. All major publishers issue regular catalogues, and the latest productions from Bowker, Libraries Unlimited, Library Association Publishing/Clive Bingley, Gower Publishing, and relevant professional associations such as Aslib will reveal a good selection.

Newsletters: Newsletters are issued in serial format and provide up-to-date information on current activities and initiatives. They are generally slight in size and may be produced to a lower standard than normal journals. Because they are produced for speedy circulation, they may not carry volume and part numbers, but only a date of issue. Material of long-term value will normally appear in a more substantial form in a journal article, or report, at a later date, the publishers of newsletters do not produce them with an eye to their permanent retention in libraries, although this often does happen.

J. R. Sharp and M. Mann have compiled *A select list of newsletters in the field of librarianship and information science* (British Library Research and Development Department report no. 5630. 1981); although this includes only English-language material, and specifically excludes newsletters issued by individual libraries, subdivisions of national library associations, associations covering a limited region, and co-operative schemes, yet the total number recorded is over one hundred. If we include all the other categories, clearly a formidable industry is at work here.

We shall first mention newsletters issued by professional associations; the American Library Association issues *American Libraries*, but supplements this with the *ALA Washington Newsletter* reporting current governmental activity. Divisions of the American Library Associations are responsible for many newsletters, ranging from substantial items such as the *Newsletter on Intellectual Freedom* (issued bimonthly by the ALA Office for Intellectual Freedom) which reports national and state legislation, individual court proceedings, specific controversial books, newspapers, magazines, posters, games, films and television programmes, and does not confine itself to North American activity, to rather slimmer titles, for example *LITA Newsletter* (issued by the ALA Library and Information Technology Association) or *RASD Update*, (issued bimonthly by the ALA Reference and Adult Services Division).

In the United Kingdom, the Library Association has changed the format of the *Record* to carry more newsletter-type material, and its monthly production facilitates this. The various groups of the Association issue newsletters which record current activity in their field; often, for financial reasons, these do not appear as frequently as the demand for currency would dictate. Titles vary from those groups covering types of library – *UCR Newsletter* (from the University, College and Research Section), or *Colleges of Further and Higher Education Group Bulletin*, to special interest groups – *ITs News* from the Information Technology Group, *Training and Education* from the Training and Education Group, or *Public Eye* from the Publicity and Public Relations Group.

Most of the regional branches of the Library Association issue newsletters to their local members; these vary enormously in style, size and frequency; in the United States the various State library associations issue their own journals, which range from substantial serials to the simplest of newsletters.

The American Society for Information Science issues a bimonthly *Bulletin* which supplements its *Journal* but is nevertheless of high quality among newsletters; Aslib produces the monthly *Aslib Information* and the bimonthly *Netlink*. The Institute of Information Scientists publishes *Inform* each month, and has incorporated the diary section into its page of PRESTEL.

Internationally, IFLA is active in publishing newsletters; they range from *Inspel* which is a conventional journal produced by the Division for Special Libraries, to simple duplicated sheets on headed notepaper, such as the newsletters of the Section of Public Libraries, Section on School Libraries, Section of Art Libraries, or Section on Library Schools and other Training aspects. Most of these appear irregularly, and can be difficult to locate and obtain. FID produces a monthly *News Bulletin*.

A second main group of newsletter publishers consists of national library authorities, library-support groups, and related government agencies. We have already mentioned the Unesco *General Information Programme/UNISIST Newsletter* and the weekly NTIS *Library and Information Sciences* bulletin; of a similar nature are *Irish Library News* issued by the Irish Library Council, or the *Library of Congress Information Bulletin*. The Council on Library Resources Inc. provides up-to-date information in its newsletter *Recent Developments*, and

NFAIS Newsletter is published by the National Federation of Abstracting and Information Services.

In the United Kingdom, the British Library is responsible for several titles: various divisions each issue their own publications, for example *Library Conservation News* from the Preservation Office, *PIN Bulletin* from the Science Reference and Information Service Industrial Property Section, or *British Library Research and Development Newsletter*. This last Department is the body responsible for the Information Officers established under their sponsorship in a number of centres; these Officers also issue valuable newsletters recording developments in their field of activity – a list of the Officers appears on an introductory page of each issue of *CRILIS*.

Many libraries are also publishers of their own in-house newsletters, usually intended primarily for their own staff, but of value to 'outsiders' where they record new developments in active library systems. Trades unions may also produce newsletters at national, regional or local level.

Commercial publishers are also of course at work in this area; in the United States *Library Journal* and *Wilson Library Bulletin* are produced and distributed efficiently, the former fortnightly which makes it particularly good at producing current information. To supplement this, and the *School Library Journal*, Bowker also issues *Library Hotline*, which appears each Monday with the latest news of interest to librarians.

In the United Kingdom, Alan Armstrong & Associates Ltd. publishes the monthly *Library and Information News*, which carries dozens of brief paragraphs of useful information. *New Library World*, which also appears monthly, contains excellent news coverage, especially in the special sections headed 'Community Information' and 'Commercial and Technical'.

Newsletters show their greatest proliferation and their greatest use in fields which are developing rapidly. Here, new services are offered almost daily and to survive in these fields and get the best value from expensive equipment staff have to ensure that they receive up-to-the minute information; serials such as *Database, Online, Online Review, Program* or *Vine* are useful in collecting together such new information. Individual database providers generally produce news-sheets for their subscribers, and network agencies likewise issue regular bulletins to participants: the *OCLC Newsletter* is an example.

In similar vein, Knowledge Industry Publications Inc. produces *Advanced Technology/Libraries*, reporting on a range of issues in automation and electronic publishing; the Special Libraries Association publishes *SpeciaList*, which provides brief news items of interest to information workers; Lomond Publications Inc. produces *Information Retrieval and Library Automation*, reporting on equipment, software, media innovation, events, meetings and case experience; and the National Federation of Abstracting and Information Services publishes *NFAIS Newsletter*, mentioned earlier, which provides news of databases and automated abstracting over all subject fields. Useful titles are *Small Computers in Libraries* from Meckler Publishing, or *Library Hi-Tech News* sponsored by Information Society Inc. and published by Pierian Press.

For video, videotex and electronic publishing valuable items are *Cable Libraries*, produced by C.S. Tepfer Publishing Co. Inc., and *Communication Technology Impact (CTI)* from PIRA, the Research Association for the Paper and Board, Printing and Packaging Industries, and published by Elsevier International Bulletins. *CTI* covers fields of vital importance to information scientists, and its range is demonstrated by the cover page of a recent issue (Figure 10.1).

Aslib's *Netlink*, which appears bimonthly, specializes in the topic of local area networks (LANs) – an example of further fragmentation to meet new demands.

The possible full list of titles of updating services such as those mentioned would be endless; new publications are appearing regularly, and the librarian or information worker who wishes to remain abreast of new developments must search for relevant newsletters in their field, and in related fields. For more general coverage a useful source might be *Current Contents/Social and Behavioural Sciences* (Institute for Scientific Information, Philadelphia), or *Library Currents* from Practical Perspectives Inc. For non-English-language publishing *SPEL*, the College of Librarianship Wales Translation Service's quarterly bulletin of summaries of selected foreign language books and articles, might be of assistance.

Current awareness services: In addition to newsletters, some publications are issued which are designed solely to provide current information, in a readily digestible form, to professional staff in a wide area of work. Unlike specialized newsletters they are intended to appeal to all interests within certain limitations.

We have already briefly mentioned *Aslib Information*; this is supplied free to members of Aslib, but is available on subscription to others. It includes a calendar section giving brief details of forthcoming meetings and conferences, a commentary on current developments from the Aslib director, several pages of news items, and reports on meetings and events. Aslib's monthly *Current Awareness Bulletin* reviews new publications, both books and journal articles, under clear subject headings. Members can obtain items from the Aslib Library, which is the source from which the information is taken. Report literature appropriate to the special library is also included, and some items found in the more general press.

Information Hotline is published monthly by Science Associates International Inc.; although heavily United States-biased, it does aim to provide an international coverage, and includes information from European and East European sources. Its main sequence of pages is devoted to paragraphs of news information covering libraries, information units, computing, and a wide variety of fields of concern to their staffs. In addition to some twenty or more pages of this kind of information in each issue, it carries a number of useful appendices: these include details of new National Science Foundation grants and contracts, at regular intervals new British Library grants, 'non-critical descriptions of new information-related publications', details of forthcoming courses and conferences, several pages recording new NTIS reports with brief abstracts, and titles and authors of papers delivered at recent conferences in the information field. *Information Hotline* is an excellent source of current US information; it is exemplary in its coverage and currency, but unfortunately not as international as it could be.

A British equivalent is *CABLIS* – the acronym stands for Current Awareness Bulletin for Librarians and Information Scientists – which is produced monthly, and first appeared in 1976. Initially it was an internal British Library service, but now it is available on subscription to anyone. It is compiled in the Library Association Library, which is a part of the British Library Public Services, Humanities and Social

FIGURE 10.1

Volume 8 Number 5 AUGUST 1986

ISSN 0142-5854

CTI COMMUNICATION TECHNOLOGY IMPACT

AN INTERNATIONAL BULLETIN FOR PUBLISHERS AND INFORMATION HANDLING ORGANISATIONS

Editor:
Tony Powell

EDITORIAL ADVISORS:

Michael Bruno, Graphic Arts Consultant, USA. **Dr. T. H. Cannon**, British National Bibliography Research Fund, UK. **Tony Cawkell**, Managing Director, Citech Ltd, UK. **Eric Davies**, University of Loughborough, UK. **Peter Ferris**, Information Systems Director, John Wiley, UK. **Prof. W. Gosling**, Plessey, UK. **John Martyn**, British National Bibliography Research Fund, UK. **John Senders**, University of Maine, USA. **Dr. R. K. Summit**, Lockheed Dialog, USA. **Bernard Williams**, Director, Cimtech, UK. **David R. Worlock**, Director, EPS, UK.

CONTENTS

CD-ROM SPECIAL!

The ADONIS document delivery service (see CTI vol 4 no 7 page 1)
has emerged from its period of hibernation. On 2 July 1986 the
ADONIS Board authorized a series of tests during the next two and a
half years in the field of document delivery. The experimental
service will be based on biomedical literature and will use CD-ROM
in mixed mode.

The original ADONIS service was expected to deliver the text of
articles (including graphics, etc) of 3500 scientific, technical
and medical (STM) journals to large document delivery centres. The
printed journals would be scanned and the contents written on to
large (30 cm) digital optical disks.

In 1980 and 1983 surveys of what journals were most heavily copied
at the British Library Lending Division in Boston Spa (now the
British Library Document Supply Centre - BLDSC) had shown that the
most heavily requested articles were biomedical and up to two years
old. This was confirmed also in the 1985 ICSTI survey of five
major centres.

The original ADONIS concept was based on the hypothesis that if new
technology could be used to fulfil requests cheaper than the
current labour intensive photocopying procedures, the savings could
be shared with publishers without substantially changing the price
the libraries charged for documents.

**LATEST NEWS ON
ADONIS**

**COMMUNICATION
TECHNOLOGY
IMPACT**

Sciences, and is based on books and journals arriving in the Library. The opening pages of each issue feature paragraphs of brief news items, with a source indicated for further information. The subject field is wider than *Information Hotline*, with good coverage of traditional librarianship, publishing and bookselling topics, as well as information handling and automation. There is wide coverage of international material. A specimen page is reproduced here (Figure 10.2) to show format, style and references.

There then follows a section devoted to new books: brief descriptive notes are given for every title (Figure 10.3) and here again coverage of subjects is wide, and sources are international. Contents lists of a selection of newly issued journals form a further section followed by Conference proceedings – Figure 10.4 shows the layout of both these sections. *CABLIS* also includes a list of new books added to the Library, arranged by broad subjects, and a small number of abstracts to theses.

A valuable 'alternative' view of the profession can be seen through such publications as the US *Unabashed Librarian* or *WILpower*, newsletter of 'Women in Libraries'.

Information contacts: We have mentioned when discussing newsletters and research that the British Library Research and Development Department has sponsored a number of Information Officers with special responsibilities for a number of rapidly expanding topics, and these are listed in each issue of *CRILIS*. The role of these Officers is to collect and disseminate information on developments in their field, and they should be used as contacts to provide information directly if their newsletters have not provided quite the data required, or have reported activity that needs to be followed up by personal visits or discussion. The amount of material gathered by the Officers, both as written reports and as oral comment by those they meet, is formidable, and those who have a genuine need for the latest information and cannot easily find it in published form should definitely make a personal approach.

Outside the United Kingdom, the national library association or information scientists' association will be the best first contact to advise on individuals with the latest knowledge. In recent years information consultants have appeared in the profession; for a fee a consultant will examine a library, a system or a particular problem and produce a report outlining the various courses of action open to fulfil specified needs or meet specified cost targets.

In the United States the ERIC network comprises sixteen clearinghouses, and several of these will be of relevance to our profession; these include Educational Management, Higher Education, Information Resources, Reading and Communication Skills, Social Sciences/Social Science Education. Individual clearinghouses may be able to provide direct assistance or names of contacts in instances where published material is insufficient. A full list with addresses appears inside the rear cover of each issue of *Resources in Education*.

A further source of up-to-date information is the conference, seminar or workshop; contacts made at such events are on two levels: informal, social contact can provide much valuable off-the-record data on new products or systems, while the papers presented should represent the latest position as seen by experts in the field. This being so, it is regrettable that bibliographical control of conference papers is very poor; major national meetings may have papers published, but sometimes even this can be unreliable, and may include only plenary sessions and not smaller meetings. Papers may be published as audiotapes, particularly frustrating if no adequate indexing or editing procedure has been followed. Guy Marco describes coverage as 'dismal' and points out that papers are regularly 'lost to bibliographic control, and thus to the profession at large' (Marco, 1983).

The only solution to those committed to a specific area of activity is assiduously to monitor conference proceedings in their field, either by attendance or by informal contact with organizing bodies, to discover titles of papers and identities of participants.

Directories and guides: In rapidly developing areas information should also be sought from commercially produced directories and guides. These will not only provide up-to-date information on products and services, but will also reveal identities of existing users and user groups, who may be able to share advice and experiences. An example of such a directory is A.T. Kruzas and J. Schmittroth's *Encyclopedia of Information Systems and Services* 1985/86 (Gale Research, 1986) which lists computer-readable databases and their producers and publishers, vendors, networks, time-sharing agencies and teletext/videotext systems. There is a section on fee-based

FIGURE 10.2

4 CABLIS November 1986

PERGAMON ACQUIRES SDC SEARCH SERVICE

The Systems Development Corporation (SDC) now owned by Burroughs was, in the early days of online a world leader, its Orbit software and General Manager Carlos Cuadra being the chief rivals of Dialog and its Roger Summit.

Now the files, disk drives and rights and the name Orbit Information Technologies Corporation have been acquired by Mr Maxwell's Pergamon-Infoline(P.I) for an undisclosed sum. Also unknown is whether the files at present mounted on Orbit will be transferred to P-I's Basis.

Source: (among others): Monitor (67) September 1986, pp.1-2

NCLIS CHAIR?

Source: National library news 18(9) September 1986, p.6

NEW TECHNOLOGY

CD-I FOR CHRISTMAS 1987?

The development of the Compact Disc-Interactive(CD-I) which, it is hoped, may be available in the shops by the end of next year, is foreseen as bringing closer frequent home use of abstracting and indexing services. While many online hosts (mainly in the USA) already offer incentives for home use via personal computers, it is suggested that other home uses for CD-I(audio and video) will rapidly bring prices down to a level where individuals may buy databases in this format - or use borrowed ones.

Meanwhile LA Publishing Ltd has announced that Library and Information Science Abstracts(LISA) from 1969

Libraries and Information Science
(NCLIS) remain obscure. We read of
zero budgets; we observe directors
at international conferences; we
note that there is another White
House Conference(WHCLIS) in the
offing (funds permitting).

Meanwhile President Reagan is quoted
as awarding the chair to a Readers
Digest Chief: Kenneth Y Tomlinson
is to replace Elinor M Hashin of
OCLC. NCLIS director - to replace
Toni Carbo Bearman - (now Dean of
Pittsburg SLIS) - is unlikely to be
agreed until Mr Tomlinson has
senate approval. He is said to be
'close to the White House'.

Source: Library journal 111(14)
September 1986, p.131

CANADIAN CONCENTRATION OF IT

The National Library of Canada is
to combine its Library Systems
Centre, the office for Network
Development and strategic systems
planning into a single new organisation to be known as Information
Technology.

also be an option of outright
purchase @ $4995 for 1969-86. It
is understood that Newcastle Polytechnic library school has entered
a firm subscription.

Sources: Information intelligence
online newsletter 7(10) October
1986, p.8 and Information world
review (7) September 1986, p.3.

WILL SCANNERS AND PC'S REPLACE FAX?

As word-processing (and desk-top
publishing?) increasingly move on
to personal computers (PC's) there
is a suggestion that, given trans-
parent software, the new range of
scanners might make PC's a cost-
effective alternative to Group 3
facsimile(FAX). A market research
report from the prolific International
Resource Development (Connecticut
USA) forecasts that by 1988 "virtual
facsimile" sales will outstrip
traditional sales and by 1991 the
units of each type in use will be
equal (both US figures).

Source: The International communications report (5/4) September 1986,
pp.1-2 and p.8

FIGURE 10.3

'CABLIS November 1986 7

Cullen, Patsy
Design and production of media presentations for libraries/ Patsy Cullen and John Kirby. Aldershot: Gower, c1986. ix,83p
ISBN 0-566-03548-0 £21.45
  Shelf mark: **021.7 CUL**
A basic guide, full of checklists and examples, aimed to assist the beginner as well as reminding others of the need for clear objectives, realistic timescales and measures for evaluation.

Heynen, Jeffrey
The CONSER project: recommendations for the future: report of a study conducted for the Library of Congress/by Jeffrey Heynen and Julia C. Blixrud. Washington: Serial Record Division, Processing Services, Library of Congress, 1986. ix, 122p

This first of a new series opens with a general section on briefs, clients and professionals and then moves on to specific library topics. Appendices include lists of references, addresses (UK & US) photographs and a consideration of alternative means of developing a brief.

Liu, Songfu
A design for library user education for scientists and engineers in China/Liu Songfu. Göteborg: Chalmers Tekniska Högskola, Biblioteket, 1984. 48 leaves. (CTHB publikation; nr. 34) £9.69
  Shelf mark: **025.560951 LIU**
The report of a two-year secondment from the Chongqing Branch of the Institute of Scientific and Technical Information of China to the Chalmers University of Technology

to study interlending systems in the UK.

Part III a preliminary design, has a map and some detailed facts and figures on the educational system of the People's Republic.

...years after this series conversion project started, it seemed appropriate to review progress and suggest future developments. The Recommendations are addressed to CONSER's participants and Advisory Groups and are summarised in Appendix G.

Industrial and commercial libraries: an introductory guide/Library Association Industrial Group. London: Library Association, 1986. viii, 44p. (Library Association pamphlet; 39) ISBN 0-85365-577-4 Shelf mark: **027.69 IND**

A basic introduction for managers and library staff, emphasising the types of speciality required. Further reading and points of contact are included.

Konya, Allan
Libraries: a briefing and design guide. London: Architectural Press, 1986. 182p. (Briefing and design guides; 1) ISBN 0-85139-765-4 Shelf mark: **727.8 KON**

Martin, Susan K.
Library networks, 1986-87: libraries in partnership. White Plains, NY. London: Knowledge Industry Publications, c1986. x, 251p (Professional librarian series) ISBN 0-86729-128-1 £36.25 Shelf mark: **021.65 MAR**

A complete revision of an earlier standard text originally entitled Library network 1976-77. The American bias is pronounced: the only mentions of UK bodies are of the British Library as a source of records and joint sponsor of a conference.

Maslin, J. M.
Non-impact printing: developments and applications/J. M. Maslin and A. W. Davies. Oxford: Elsevier International Bulletins, c1986. iv, 100p. ISBN

FIGURE 10.4

CABLIS November 1986 17

Impact of optical disc technologies on the storage and distribution of patent and trademark information / M S White, 177-181

Computerisation of the United Kingdom Patent Office / R J Marchant, 182-184

The Patent Office databases on Pergamon InfoLine / C Oppenheim, 185-192

Intellectual property and innovation: a comment on the United Kingdom White Paper on patent law reform / J Phillips, 193-197

Patent information services of the Swiss Federal Intellectual Property Office(SIPO) / H Evers, 198-205

G. D. R. patent information system promotes the creation of modern high technologies as well as of complex innovation processes / J Hemmerling, 206-209

JAPIO, the paperless Plan of the Japanese Patent Office, 210-217

Online patent information. / S M Kaback, 218-219

Mixed signals and painful choices: the education of special librarians / Marion Paris, Herbert S White, 207-212

What corporate librarians will need to know in the future / Mary J Culnan, 213-216

Changes in library education: the deans reply / 217-225

The Scholarship program: still a good use of SLA funds? / Muriel Regan, 226-229

Accreditation: a blueprint for action / Vivian J Arterbery, 230-234

*TDR 9(9) September 1986

Computer services trade evolves, 5-6

UK Data Flow Regulations, 6

Right to know in Canada / Inger Hansen, 11-12

Controlling International Information Economy Conflicts / Klaus W Grewlich, 13-15

Towards a Universal Data Flow Order. Universal legal regime achievable? / Leila Bouachera, 16-18

TDR 9(10) October 1986

Restructuring S.W.I.F.T., 5-6

Singapore moving into the information age / Yeo Khee Leng, 14-15

UK data protection: overcoming confusion / J J Kenny, 17

Automation and non-professional staff at the Polytechnic of the South Bank / Philip Sykes, 50-56

Computer assisted learning in the teaching of library management / John Hall, 57-61

TREFFPUNKT BIBLIOTHEK 3(3) 1986
Wieviel Medien braucht der Mensch? / Urs Jaeggi, 7-14
Klassenleseserien für die Kantone Zürich und Thurgau / Richard Burgisser, 15-18

VINE (63) August 1986
ACCLAIM at Derbyshire [an inhouse system], 4-13
CAFS as a University Library catalogue search facility / J L Beck. J D Craig, 14-20
CATS - a machine independent online catalogue system [Cambridge] / W D S Motherwell, 21-25
Automation in the University of London / V T H Parry, 26-27
Remote access to OPACs and the use of electronic mail in university libraries" / Peter Stone, 28-30
CAG Steering Group: achievements to date, 31-35
Quartet: a collaborative research project in digital information interchange / Bill Tuck, 36-41

WORLD PATENT INFORMATION 8(3) 1986
Rapid patent service: delivering patent information / H B Greenway. C J Merek, 171-174
Patents and CD-ROM / R Notman-Watt, 175-176

CONFERENCES ETC

Education for professional librarians/edited by Herbert S. White. White Plains. NY. London: Knowledge Industry Publications. c1986. xii. 287p. (Professional librarian series) ISBN 0-86729-197-4. £36.25 Shelf mark: 020.7 EDU

Practitioner expectations and needs
University research libraries / Sheila D Creth, 3-26
Large public libraries / Donald J Sager, 27-48
College libraries / Evan Ira Farber, 49-65
Small public libraries / Sara Laughlin, 67-88
Corporate libraries / Elin B Christianson, 89-103
Medical libraries / Erika Love, 105-122
School libraries and media centers / Karen K Niemeyer, 123-139
Federal government libraries and information centers / Patricia W Berger, 141-153
The Information industry / Herbert R Brinberg, 155-169

Educational preparation programs
Graduate education for the library profession / Herbert S White, 173-199
The Role of the undergraduate library education program / Ronald Bryson, 201-221
Continuing education programs and activities / Darlene E Weingand, 223-235
The View of the student / Louise D Schlesinger, 237-250

information services, and referral centres and clearinghouses. Between editions of the *Encyclopedia* a periodical supplement is published, entitled *New Information Systems and Services*.

Another directory regularly updated is Susan K. Martin's *Library Networks, 1986–87* (Knowledge Industry Publications, 1986) which discusses the current situation in general, gives information on hardware and software, and forecasts future developments on networking. The second half of the volume is a directory of US networks giving locations, status, plans, and lists of members.

Further news of online services is available in R. N. Cuadra's *Directory of on-line databases* (Cuadra/Elsevier); this is published four times per year – two issues of the full directory and two updates. It lists databases with full descriptions, and gives information on producers and online services.

For British services there is J. L. Hall and M. J. Brown's *Online bibliographic databases*, (4th ed., Aslib, 1986) which includes a definitive bibliography of over one thousand items. Another new service is *BRIT-LINE: a directory of British databases* (Educational Data Information Ltd [EDI] 1986), which carries useful explanations of electronic mail.

Much trade literature is available on equipment and services; this is sometimes more conveniently traced through buyers' guides and similar compendia. For example the American Library Association issues *Library Technology Reports* six times per year, giving details of new products; a retrospective cumulation is available – *Sourcebook of Library Technology: a cumulative edition of library technology reports 1965–1980* – with a printed contents list and index and a set of microfiche of the reports themselves. Audio-visual hardware is included, also theft detection equipment, word processors, lighting and furniture. Out-of-date reports are removed, but prices are left unrevised.

Reviews of new publications: A final route to new information is the monitoring of new monographs and reports, the value of which is at their greatest when they are newly published. Many professional journals carry reviews, and the speed of their appearance varies enormously. In Great Britain, the *Library Association Record* carries a relatively small number of reviews, and needs to be supplemented by scanning specialist journals and newsletters. For the United States *Library Journal*'s 'professional reading' pages and *Wilson Library Bulletin*'s 'our profession' and 'marketplace' features are prompt in reviewing new titles of a general professional interest, and there are large numbers of specialist journals active in their own areas. *College and Research Libraries* reviews widely in fields of interest to its readers; a section notifying recent publications is followed by many book reviews of a high standard, by established experts, and usually brief and concise. There are also abstracts of new ERIC reports. From 1983 *CLR* also carries a valuable series of critical reviews of journals.

The *Journal of Academic Librarianship* is a particularly useful source of review material: in addition to several pages of book reviews, it carries a guide to new books and book reviews that have appeared in recent issues of other journals. This is an extremely convenient and yet thorough means of retaining an awareness of new publishing in our professional areas.

The section 'librarians' bookshelf' in *Bowker Annual* and parts of *American Reference Books Annual* (Libraries Unlimited) carry useful synopses of important items. By far the most comprehensive and thorough annual summary of new professional publishing is found in the new *Library Science Annual*, discussed earlier in this chapter. This volume intends to expand its present North American coverage to include all English-language library science titles published worldwide.

References and bibliography

Ali, S.N., 'Library and information science literature: research results', *International Library Review*, 1985, vol.17, no.2, pp.117–28.

Anthony, A., Weiner, S. and Eden, V., 'Examination of search strategy and an on-line bibliographic system pertaining to library and information sciences', *Special Libraries*, 1979, vol.70, no.3, pp.127–34.

Bakewell, K.G.B., 'Indexing *LISA*', *Indexer*, 1983, vol.13, no.4, pp.261–4.

Berman, S., 'Alternative library lit.', *Library Journal*, 1978, vol.103, no.1, pp.23–5.

Bottle, R.T., 'Literature of library and information science: a review article', *Journal of Librarianship*, 1985, vol.17, no.1, pp.49–53.

Bottle, R.T. and Efthimiadis, E.N., 'Library and information science literature: authorship and growth patterns', *Journal of Information Science*, 1984, vol.9, no.3, pp.107–16.

Buckley, B.J., 'Coverage of library/information science periodicals from developing countries', *IFLA Journal*, 1982, vol.8, no.4, pp.379–87.

Champlin, P., 'The on-line search; some perils and pitfalls', *RQ*, 1985, vol.25, no.2, pp.213–17.

Coates, E.J., 'Switching languages for indexing', *Journal of Documentation*, 1970, vol.26, no.2, pp.102–10.

Coblans, H., 'Progress in documentation. The literature of librarianship and documentation: the periodicals and their control', *Journal of Documentation*, 1972, vol. 28, no. 1, pp. 56–66.

Danky, J.P. and Fox, M., 'Alternative periodicals', *Wilson Library Bulletin*, 1977, vol. 51, no. 9, pp. 763–8.

Dansey, P., 'A bibliometric survey of primary and secondary information science literature', *Aslib Proceedings*, 1973, vol. 25, no. 7, pp. 252–63.

Edwards, T., *A comparative analysis of the major abstracting and indexing services for library and information science*, Paris, Unesco, 1975. (A condensed version appears in *Unesco Bullletin for Libraries*, 1976, vol. 30, no. 1, pp. 18–25.

Gilchrist, A., 'Documentation of documentation: a survey of leading abstracts services in documentation and an identification of key journals', *Aslib Proceedings*, 1966, vol. 18, no. 3, pp. 62–80.

Goldstein, S., 'Statistical bibliography and library periodical literature – part 4', *CALL*, 1973, vol. 2, no. 4, pp. 3–13.

Goldstein, S., 'Using the literature of librarianship', *CALL*, 1979, vol. 8, no. 1, pp. 11–14.

Gresham, J., 'The abandoned switchboard: library/information journals', *Library Review*, 1979, vol. 28, no. 3, pp. 143–7.

Hardesty, L. 'Use of slide–tape presentations in academic libraries: a state-of-the-art survey', *Journal of Academic Librarianship*, 1977, vol. 3, no. 3, pp. 134–40.

Johnson, R.D., 'Journal literature of librarianship', in *Advances in librarianship*, no. 12, Academic Press, 1982, pp. 127–50.

Jones, G., 'This incredible stream of garbage: the library journals, 1876–1975', *Indexer*, 1976, vol. 10, no. 1, pp. 9–14.

Kent, A., 'Is *ELIS* worthy of the name?', *Wilson Library Bulletin*, 1973, vol. 47, no. 7, pp. 602–4.

Kister, K., '"ELIS" in progress', *Library Journal*, 1981, vol. 106, no. 10, p. 1051.

Knapp, S. D. and Zych, M. L., 'The ERIC data base and the literature of library and information science', *RQ*, 1977, vol. 16, no. 3, pp. 209–12.

Krausse, S. C. and Sieburth, J. F., 'Patterns of authorship in library journals by academic librarians', *Serials Librarian*, 1985, vol. 9, no. 3, pp. 127–38.

LaBorie, T., 'Publishing in library journals', *Serials Librarian*, 1984, vol. 8, no. 3, pp. 55–61.

LaBorie, T., Halperin, M. and White, H. D., 'Library and information science abstracting and indexing services', *Library and Information Research*, 1985, vol. 7, no. 2, pp. 183–95.

Lee, J. M., 'Collections in librarianship and information science', *Drexel Library Quarterly*, 1979, vol. 15, no. 3, pp. 78–94.

Library Association, *Library and Information Bulletin*, 1970 (no. 9), 1971 (no. 16), and 1974 (no. 24).

Library Association, *Library Association Record*, 1979, vol. 81, no. 4, p. 205.

Lilley, D. B. and Badough, R. M., *Library and information science: a guide to information sources*, Gale Research, 1982.

McElroy, A. R., [letter] 'Linguistic librarianship', *Library Association Record*, 1979, vol. 81, no. 7, p. 349.

Marco, G. A., 'Bibliographic control of library and information science literature', *Libri*, 1983, vol. 33, no. 1, pp. 45–60.

Moon, E., 'Dullness and duplications', *Library Journal*, 1961, vol. 86, no. 15, p. 2760.

Moon, E., 'The library press', *Library Journal*, 1969, vol. 94, no. 20, pp. 4104–9.

Moore, N., 'Library periodicals from developing countries', *Journal of Librarianship*, 1981, vol. 13, no. 1, pp. 37–45.

O'Connor, D. and Van Orden, P., 'Getting into print', *College and Research Libraries*, 1978, vol. 39, no. 5, pp. 389–96.

O'Leary, M., 'WILSEARCH: a new departure for an old institution', *Online*, 1986, vol. 10, no. 2. pp. 102–7.

Ollé, J. G., 'British books on librarianship', *British Book News*, 1981 (March), pp. 133–9.

Palmer, J. W., 'Non-print media about librarianship and information science', *Drexel Library Quarterly*, 1979, vol. 15, no. 3, pp. 52–76.

Peritz, B. C., 'Citation characteristics in library science', *Library Research*, 1981, vol. 3, no. 1, pp. 47–65.

Prytherch, R. J. and Satija, M. P., 'Indian library and information science literature: a guide to its coverage and control', *Libri*, 1986, vol. 36, no. 2, pp. 163–86.

Purcell, G. R. and Schlachter, G. A., *Reference sources in library and information services*, ABC-Clio, 1984.

Richardson, J. V., 'Readability and readership of journals in library science', *Journal of Academic Librarianship*, 1977, vol. 3, no. 1, pp. 20–2.

Roberts, N., '10 years of library journals in Great Britain, 1969–1979', *Journal of Librarianship*, 1979, vol. 11, no. 3, pp. 163–82.

Rosenberg, L. and Detlefsen, G., 'Is *ELIS* worthy of the name?', *Wilson Library Bulletin*, 1973, vol. 47, no. 7, pp. 598–601.

Schuman, P. G. and Pedolsky, A., 'Publishers of library science books and monographs', *Drexel Library Quarterly*, 1979, vol. 15, no. 3, pp. 77–98.

Seaton, J., 'Readability tests for U.K. professional journals', *Journal of Librarianship*, 1975, vol. 7, no. 2, pp. 69–83.

Shores, L., 'Press proliferation: a word for more', *RQ*, 1972, vol. 11, no. 4, pp. 297–9.

Stefaniak, B., 'Periodical literature of information science as reflected in *Referativnyj Zhurnal*', *Scientometrics*, 1985, vol. 7, nos. 3–6, pp. 177–94.

Stevens, N. D., 'In praise of library literature', *American Libraries*, 1984, vol. 15, no. 4, pp. 216–17.

Su, Meng-Fen, 'Current library science journals in China', *Serials Librarian*, 1984, vol. 9, no. 2, pp. 93–106.

Taylor, L. J., 'Library science literature' in H. A. Whatley, *British Librarianship and Information Science 1971–1975*, Library Association, 1977, pp. 112–121.

Taylor, L. J., 'Library science literature: some problems of information about information', *Aslib Proceedings*, 1971, vol. 23, no. 9, pp. 465–80.

Tegler, P., 'The indexes and abstracts of library and information science', *Drexel Library Quarterly*, 1979, vol. 15, no. 3, pp. 2–23.

Thompson, A., 'A note on the international terminology of documentation and libraries', *Focus on International and Comparative Librarianship*, 1975, vol. 6, no. 2, pp. 18–19 and vol. 6, no. 3, pp. 30–1.

Umapathy, K. S., 'Indian library science literature', *International Library Review*, 1981, vol. 13, no. 2, pp. 141–54.

UNISIST: study report of the feasibility of a World Science Information System, Paris, Unesco, 1971.

Wagner-Urbain, M., 'Bibliographical note on professional literature', *Journal of Library History*, 1984, vol. 19, no. 1, pp. 166–82.

Index